70855497

TRADITIONAL TOYS

OVER 20 CLASSIC DESIGNS FOR
MAKING IN WOOD

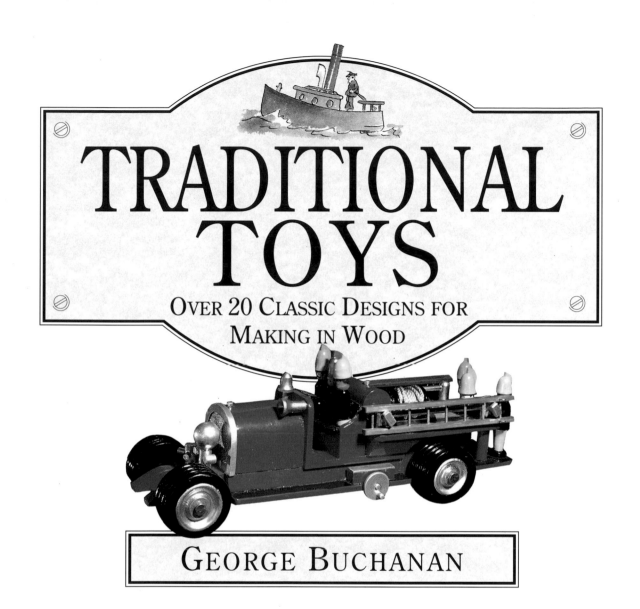

TRADITIONAL TOYS

OVER 20 CLASSIC DESIGNS FOR
MAKING IN WOOD

GEORGE BUCHANAN

BCA

LONDON NEW YORK SYDNEY TORONTO

TO MY DAD

First published in 1993 by
HarperCollins*Publishers*

This edition published 1993 by BCA by
arrangement with HarperCollins*Publishers*

CN 5858

Text and Illustrations
© George Buchanan 1993

George Buchanan reserves the moral right
to be identified as the author of this work

Editor: Richard Dawes
Designer: Rachel Smyth
Photographer: Theo Bergström
Index: Susan Bosanko

Commissioning Editor: Polly Powell
Project Editor: Barbara Dixon
Art Director: Ray Barnett

All rights reserved. No part of this
publication may be reproduced, stored in a
retrieval system, or transmitted, in any form
or by any means, electronic, mechanical,
photocopying, recording or otherwise,
without the prior written permission of
the publishers.

**A catalogue record for this book is
available from the British Library**

Colour reproduction by Colourscan,
Singapore
Printed and bound in Spain by Graficromo

CONTENTS

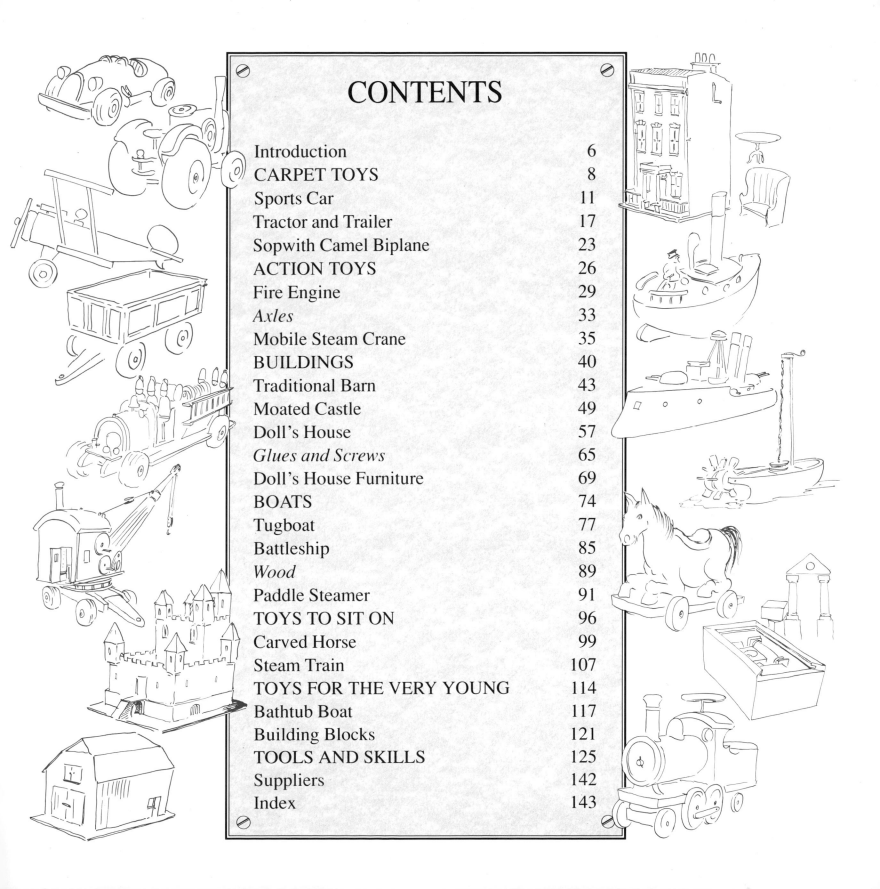

INTRODUCTION

I remember vividly Christmas morning when I was five years old. It was long before dawn, very dark outside, and cold. Our parents came into our room and hurried us to get up. We pulled on our dressing gowns and followed them into the sitting room. Before us stood two beautiful toy boats: a steam car ferry and next to it an elegant, two-funnelled paddle steamer. Dad danced about as he explained how the elastic band turned the paddle-wheels and how the ramps were lowered. He had been up all night putting the finishing touches to our presents and could not wait a minute longer to give them to us.

My brother and I were astonished. Earlier that week we had sneaked into our father's workshop, curious about why he was spending so much time there, and had seen the boats high up on his woodworking bench. The hulls were shaped and the little cabins had tiny stairs leading to them. They were magic, though we had no idea they were for us.

We have kept our boats, which are now a little the worse for wear. As designs, they had their shortcomings. My paddle steamer could never steer in a straight line and my brother's ferry, with its loading ramps and clockwork motor, was too big to carry to the pond. But as presents they were a knockout. They were an offering of devotion, for in making them our parents had given us the rich gift of their time, their imagination and their skills. To this day we both still treasure these special boats, which embody so much love and enthusiasm.

I have written this book because I would like people to share the pleasure of making and giving lovingly crafted toys. For me, toymaking is an area of creativity where the benchmark of quality is not fine joints and perfect finishes, but the invention and imagination toys stimulate, and the lasting pleasure they bring.

Detailed plans and illustrations accompany the projects in this book, and by following the instructions carefully you should be able to make a wide variety of worthwhile toys. But before you begin a project, browse through the whole book and think about incorporating or adapting features from other toys. This approach to toymaking is not only more fun, but the results will be unique and, even more important, just what you want.

I have grouped the toys into types that share a similar construction logic

– for example, carpet toys, action toys and buildings. At the back of the book there is a section intended to help those who are not familiar with using tools. This also describes the main skills you will need to acquire.

None of the toys described here is difficult to make, but you should use only good-quality tools. A tool is an extension of your arm, and using anything less than first-rate will only lead to frustration. For the projects in this book, you will need the basic selection shown on the right.

Second-hand tools are often more expensive than new ones, and if you need to buy new tools, choose simple, traditional items of the best

---

HAND TOOLS

Chisels, preferably bevel-edged: ¼in (6mm), ⅜in (9mm), ⅝in (15mm)
Gouges: No 4 (16mm), No 8 (8mm), No 10 (4mm)
Smoothing plane
Low-angle shoulder plane
Fretsaw
Tenon saw
Set square
Angle bevel
Hammers
Drills
Clamps
Vice

POWER TOOLS

Circular saw
Jigsaw
Electric drill and stand
Router and stand
Lathe

---

quality. I use an old wood-turner's lathe, crudely adapted to electric power. For those looking for a new lathe, Record make a solid, low-priced but high-quality model which is supplied with motor, face plate and tools, and I have featured this in the illustrations. As for power tools, those made by Bosch give me more of what I need in a tool than any other make I have tried, and I have used them for making all of the toys in this book.

CARPET
TOYS

SPORTS CAR

This attractive little car is pleasing to hold and easy to make. Apart from the wheels and axles, the only other moving part is the door of the rear luggage compartment, which is hinged. The car's body is mounted on a simple two-strut chassis. The engine and radiator, which are carved from a single block of pine, form the front half of the car.

The floor of the passenger and luggage compartments are made from a thin sheet of plywood, to which are glued the rear side-panels, the seat and the bulkhead behind the seats. The dashboard is cut from a small sliver of plywood which extends upwards to form the windscreens. Dowel is used for the petrol tank, exhaust silencer and tail pipe. The wheels and front headlamps are turned. *(For instructions on turning see pages 133-8.)*

MATERIALS

3in x 2in (75mm x 50mm) pine
2in x 1in (50mm x 25mm) pine
³⁄₁₆in (4mm) plywood offcut (small)
¼in (6mm) dowel
⅝in (15mm) dowel
⅞in (22mm) dowel
1½in (40mm) brass hinge

TOOLS

Pillar drill, lathe, jigsaw

1 Cut out the two chassis strips, plane them smooth and mark the positions for the holes for the back and front axles. Stack the two struts together, aligning the ends and edges, and tack them together with a couple of veneer pins. Drill the holes for the axles with a pillar drill and a brad-point drill bit to ensure that the holes are clean-cut and perpendicular.

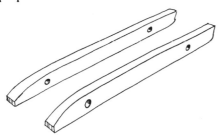

2 Cut out all the blocks for the body. Plane the back end of the engine block flat with a shoulder plane. The radiator at the front is canted at a slight angle. Mark this angle on the side of the engine block, square across with a set square and saw off the waste. Plane the front face smooth. Then plane flat and square the front edges of the side-panels, which must butt cleanly against the rear face of the engine block.

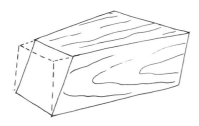

3 Mark the sweeping curve on the upper edge of each side-panel and saw or chisel off the waste. Clamp both pieces together in the vice to trim the curve and to file it smooth.

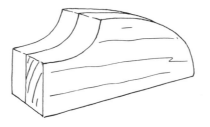

4 Saw out the floor, to which are glued the engine, the side-panels and the seat bulkhead, and cut the transverse bulkhead to length.

Assemble all the blocks. Every joint should be clean-cut and close fitting, so adjust them until they are. *(For hints on sawing and planing see pages 126-9.)* Glue the floor plate to the chassis members.

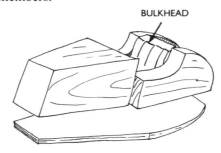

BULKHEAD

5 The car body is now ready to be assembled on the chassis. Most wood glues require some form of pressure to obtain satisfactory adhesion. Pressure, combined with the lubricating effect of the glue, often causes the components to slip out of position. To prevent this, tap two or three veneer pins into the glueing face of each component, and then snip them off, leaving them about ⅟₁₆in (2mm) proud of the surface. These will grip the pieces, and if you are careful in positioning them to begin with, will guarantee that they locate correctly.

6 Insert the front and rear axles to keep the chassis struts in alignment, and glue and pin the floor to the chassis. When the glue is dry, fit the engine block. The rear side-panels and bulkhead can all be glued in place after the engine block has been glued on.

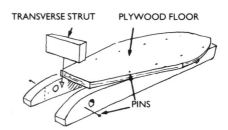

TRANSVERSE STRUT   PLYWOOD FLOOR

PINS

7 Now that the blocks are all together, they can be carved to shape. The only part missing is the lid of the luggage compartment, which is best left until later. To safeguard the edges where it fits, draw a pencil line down the side of each side-panel, to mark the areas where your chisels and sandpaper must not go.

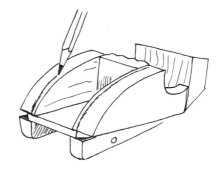

8 Use a G-clamp to hold the car to the workbench. Position the clamp in the centre of the passenger compartment and slip a piece of wood between the chassis struts to support the floor. Take a sharp ⅝in (15mm) chisel and carve the

car body in the sequence illustrated. *(For instructions on sharpening and stropping chisels see pages 130-1 and for hints on carving see pages 78-82.)* You should not have to press hard with the chisel – just take small, easy slices. Each pass of the chisel should remove its own shaving.

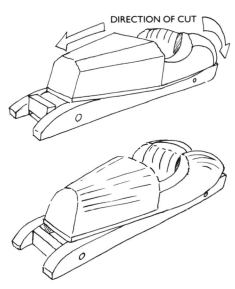

DIRECTION OF CUT

9 When you are satisfied with the body's shape, take a fresh piece of 60-grit sandpaper and holding it against a polyethlene-foam block, sand away all the chisel marks. Sand slightly across the grain and curves of the body. Do not sand over the pencil marks at the back of the car.

10 Now fit the block which will become the luggage compartment door. Plane its side until it fits between the two side-panels. Cut out a cardboard template for the two ends of the door as illustrated. Transfer the angles at each end onto the door. Saw and plane them flat. This should not be a critical operation, provided you trim and then check one end at a time.

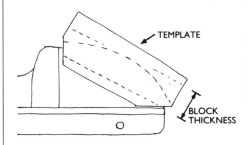

TEMPLATE

BLOCK THICKNESS

11 When you are happy with the fit, take the brass hinge and press it into position. This will wedge the door back slightly, but since you have not carved it yet, this does not matter. Mark the positions for the hinge screws on the back of the bulkhead and screw it in place.

12 Press the luggage compartment door into position and mark the exact position of the hinge. Remove the door, open the hinge and, holding the door in its open position, pencil in the centre of each screwhole. Fit one small screw, preferably not the middle screw, and tighten it. Check if the door shuts. If it does not, try shifting it a little by loosening the screw. If this fails, remove the first screw and mark the position for a new screw in the opposite end of the hinge. Because the door has not yet been

carved, its precise fit is not critical. Once you have a satisfactory fit, clamp the hinge with the central screw.

13 When the luggage compartment door is attached, close it and carve it to shape. Then sand across the rear of the car, so that the curves across the body and down the back are unbroken.

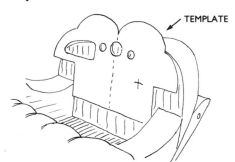

TEMPLATE

14 Make a cardboard template of the dashboard and then mark it and cut it out of the ³⁄₁₆in (4mm) plywood offcut with a fretsaw. Mark the shape of the glove compartment. Drill a small hole with a bradawl through the centre of the glove compartment. Feed the blade of the fretsaw through the hole, clamp and tension the blade and then saw round the line. *(For advice on using a fretsaw see pages 127-8.)* Glue the dashboard in position.

15 Cut out and fit the seats, carve the upholstery and sand the seats before fitting them.

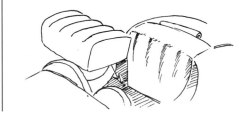

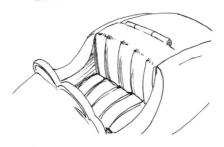

16 Fretsaw or turn the steering wheel, and fit it on the end of the short steering column. The steering column fits into an angled drill hole in

the back face of the engine block, which you can now drill.

When you are boring holes at an acute angle to the surface of the wood, and especially when you are working in a confined space, the drill has a tendency to wander. To avoid this, start with a small drill bit, about $\frac{1}{16}$in (2mm) in diameter, or a pointed nail, and then switch to the $\frac{1}{4}$in (6mm) bit once you have made the pilot hole. Do not use brad-point drills, since they will chew up the sides of the hole. It is best to use metal-working drills in these circumstances.

17 Drill and fit the exhaust system, fuel tank and back bumper. Turn and fit the headlamps. *(For advice*

relevant to turning headlamps see page 138.)

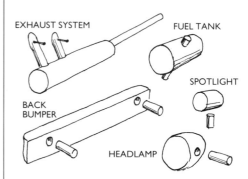

EXHAUST SYSTEM

FUEL TANK

SPOTLIGHT

BACK BUMPER

HEADLAMP

18 Fit the wheels after everything has been painted and the last coat of paint has had at least two days to harden. *(For instructions on fitting wheels see page 33.)*

DOWELS

CUTTING
Cut dowels of up to $\frac{3}{8}$in (9mm) diameter with a penknife. Mark where you want the dowel to be cut, and place the knife hard down on the dowel at right angles to its centre line. Roll the dowel back and forth with the knife, as illustrated. This will incise the outer fibres, and the end can then be snapped off.

Saw larger dowels with a tenon

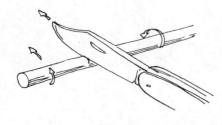

saw. Hold the dowel against the bench hook, and press lightly with the saw, otherwise the outer fibres of the dowel will splinter.

TRIMMING
Often the slightly domed top of a snapped dowel can be trimmed free hand with a chisel. If the dowel is large, or has to be planed flat, find a rectangular scrap of waste wood, and drill a perpendicular hole in it of the same diameter as the dowel. Now make a sawcut into the rectangle.

Poke the dowel into the hole, leaving one end slightly prominent. Clamp the rectangle in the vice, with its top surface slightly above the level of the vice jaws. Plane off the rough end with the block plane, as illustrated.

DRILLING
Use the pillar drill fitted with a brad-point drill. Hold the dowel between a pair of V blocks.

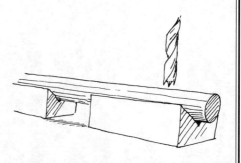

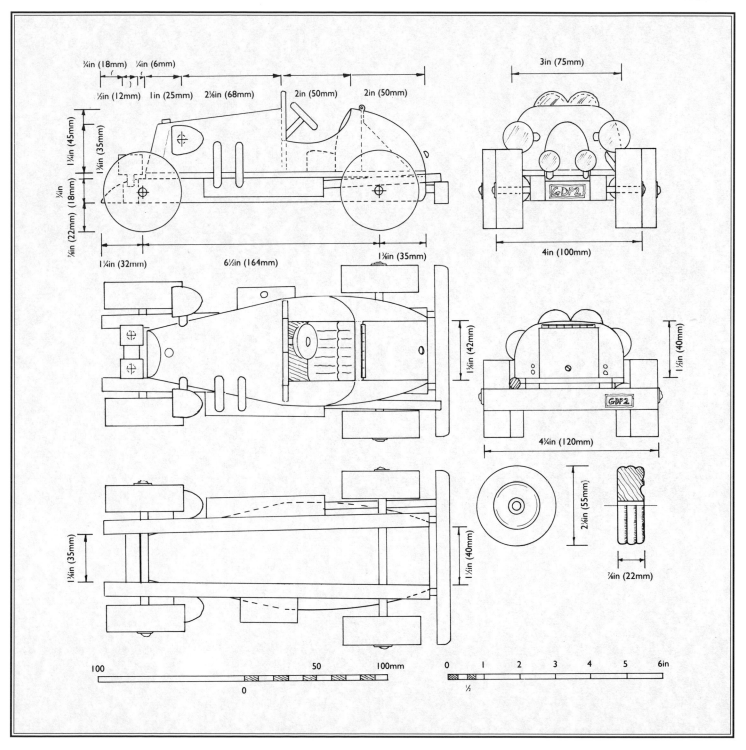

TRACTOR AND
TRAILER

The design of this tractor is based on a Field Marshal agricultural tractor. It can be steered and has a towing hook with which it can pull the trailers described below and the mobile steam crane on page 35. It is easy to make, provided the preliminary cutting and drilling are accurate. There is a choice of two trailers to make. Both are constructed on a narrow chassis. The front wheels are mounted beneath the chassis for steering. The high-sided trailer has a simple winch and gantry, over which the winch rope passes. When the winch rope is wound in, the rope lifts and empties the truck, as shown in the diagrams on page 21.

TRACTOR MATERIALS

3in x 1⅛in (75mm x 30mm) pine
¼in (6mm) dowel
⅞in (22mm) dowel
¼in (6mm) birch-faced plywood
    offcut
³⁄₁₆in (4mm) plywood offcut
3 x 2in (50mm) No 8 round-headed
    screws

TRACTOR TOOLS

Pillar drill, jigsaw, lathe

TRAILER MATERIALS

2in x 1in (50mm x 25mm) pine
½in or ⅝in x 4¾in (12mm or
    15mm x 120mm) pine
¼in (6mm) plywood
¼in (6mm) dowel
⅞in (22mm) dowel
3 x 2in (50mm) No 8 round-headed
    screws

TRAILER TOOLS

Pillar drill, lathe

TRACTOR

1 Cut out the engine block and drill the holes for the flywheel, radiator cap, front axle pivot and air intake using the pillar drill fitted with brad-point drills. Mark the slot for the steering-column support across the back of the engine block. Cut down both sides of the slot with a tenon saw and chop out the waste wood with a ¼in (6mm) chisel. Shape, drill and then fit the steering-column support. Shape the front and top of the engine and smooth its sides.

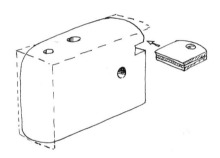

2 Cut out the rear chassis members. Tack them together, then drill the hole for the rear axle and the ¹⁄₁₆in (2mm) hole which passes through the chassis in front of the steering column. Glue the chassis members to the underside of the engine block.

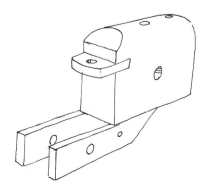

3 Cut out the plywood floor and the two blocks that fit on it. These blocks, which are the same width, fit between the rear mudguards. Glue the floor in position.

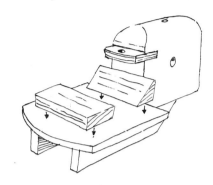

4 Make both mudguards at the same time. Each consists of a semicircle of plywood, with a pair of semicircular strips blocked together and glued to its perimeter. Note that the inner strip on the right-hand side is cut where the rubber drive belt passes from the back wheel to the flywheel pulley.

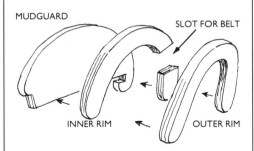

MUDGUARD   SLOT FOR BELT

INNER RIM   OUTER RIM

5 Cut out the two mudguards and the four semicircular rim strips with a fretsaw or jigsaw. Cut out the notches on the mudguards and check that they fit on the floor panel. Glue the two pairs of perimeter strips together. Cut out the slot for the belt on the right-hand rim and rub down the inside curves with 60-grit

sandpaper wrapped around the curved side of a can. Now glue the rims onto the inner semicircles and sand them smooth.

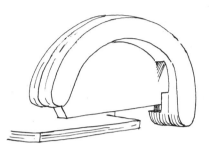

6 Fit and glue one mudguard to the floor, then glue in the two floor blocks, butting them against the first mudguard. Glue the second mudguard in place.

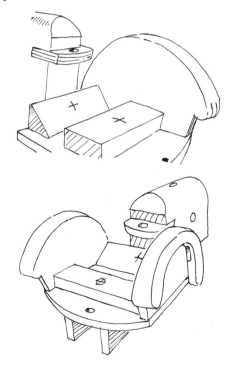

7 Use the pillar drill to bore the holes for the seat and the steering column. Clamp the tractor to the pillar drill table and drill the ¼in (6mm) seat hole with a

brad-point drill. The second hole is more critical as well as more difficult to drill cleanly. Use a metalworking drill because the footrest beneath the steering-column support is cut at an angle. If your clamping system works well for the first hole, it can probably be relied on to hold the tractor firmly while the second hole is being bored.

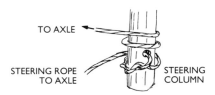

AIR INTAKE   TOWING PIN

PULLEY

AXLE

EXHAUST PIPE

FLYWHEEL

8 The remaining work is straight-forward and should not take long. *(For hints on turning wheels and pulleys see pages 133-6, and for advice on screwing and nailing see pages 65 and 131.)* Fix the front axle. Tie the end of the steering rope to one end of the front axle. Feed the rope round nail A, and beneath nail B.

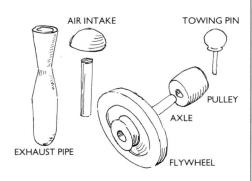

STEERING COLUMN

STEERING ROPE

B

A

FRONT AXLE

9 Press the steering column down until its end is clear of the chassis. Poke the steering rope through the hole in the steering column. Tighten the rope,

and then twist the front axle until more rope is pulled through the column. Now tie the simple thumb knot around the column, and feed it back over B, around the opposite side of A and out through the hole at the other end of the axle.

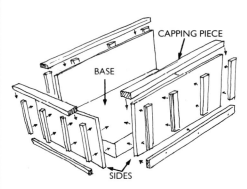

TO AXLE

STEERING ROPE TO AXLE

STEERING COLUMN

10 Turn the steering wheel to wind in the axle rope on the side that has already been fastened, and tie the remaining end. Try the steering before snipping off the ends of the steering rope and replacing the cover plate.

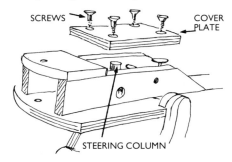

SCREWS

COVER PLATE

STEERING COLUMN

TRAILER

11 Cut out the chassis members. Trim and glue on the add-ons which hold the back axle. Tack the chassis struts together and drill the hole for the back axle. Cut and fit the two blocks which separate the chassis struts, and nail and glue them into position.

12 Make up the truck section of the trailer: this is built around the truck floor, which has been accurately sawn to shape. The front panel is then

fitted, followed by the side-panels. Glue framework struts at the bottom of the sides and front, then glue on the vertical struts. After trimming the top edges with a block plane or sharp file, fit the capping pieces. Make up the tailgate in the same way, to the dimensions shown in the plans. Cut out and fit the gantry and winch. *(For advice on using a fretsaw see pages 127-8.)*

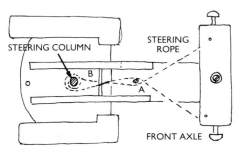

CAPPING PIECE

BASE

SIDES

13 The front axle is a simple wooden strut and the towbar is a 4in (100mm) T hinge, held to the axle with two ½in (12mm) countersunk screws, leaving the centre screw hole in the hinge for the 1½in (40mm) round-headed screw which pivots the front axle. Turn the four wheels from any close-grained hardwood. Fit the axle stop once the wheels and front axle are in position.

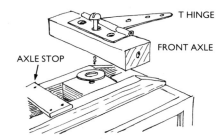

T HINGE

FRONT AXLE

AXLE STOP

Remove the T hinge, front axle and wheels before painting the trailer.

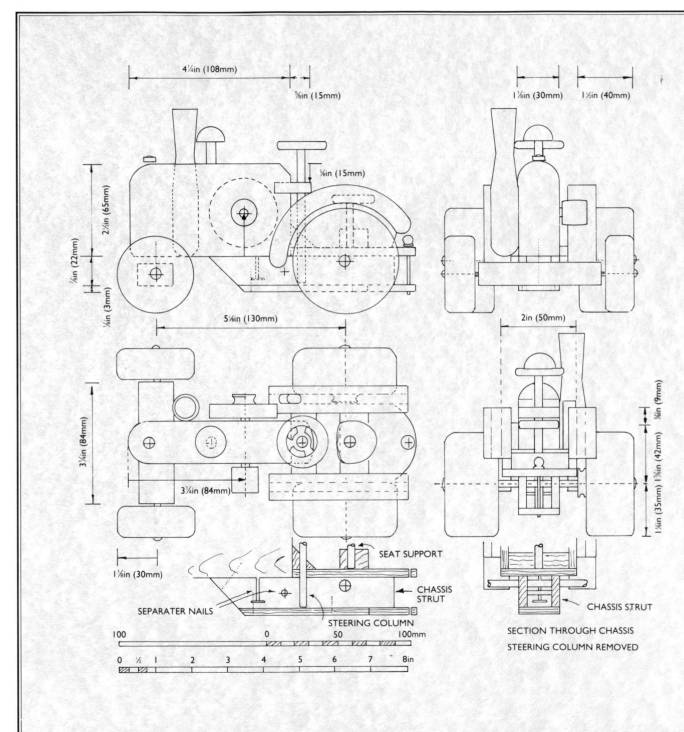

4¼in (108mm)

⅝in (15mm)

1⅛in (30mm) 1½in (40mm)

⅝in (15mm)

2½in (65mm)

⅞in (22mm)

⅛in (3mm)

5⅛in (130mm)

2in (50mm)

3¼in (84mm)

⅜in (9mm)

1⅝in (42mm)

1⅜in (35mm)

3¼in (84mm)

1⅛in (30mm)

SEPARATER NAILS

STEERING COLUMN

SEAT SUPPORT

CHASSIS
STRUT

CHASSIS STRUT

SECTION THROUGH CHASSIS
STEERING COLUMN REMOVED

100   0   50   100mm

0   ½   1   2   3   4   5   6   7   8in

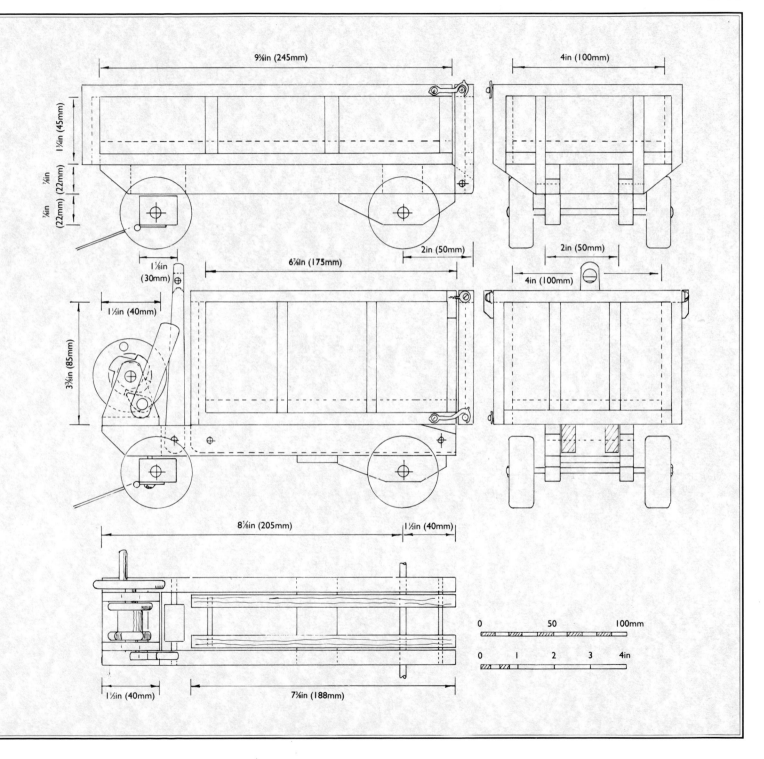

9⅝in (245mm)

4in (100mm)

1¾in (45mm)

⅞in (22mm)

⅞in (22mm)

1⅛in (30mm)

1½in (40mm)

3⅜in (85mm)

6⅞in (175mm)

2in (50mm)

2in (50mm)

4in (100mm)

8⅛in (205mm)

1½in (40mm)

1½in (40mm)

7⅜in (188mm)

0   50   100mm

0   1   2   3   4in

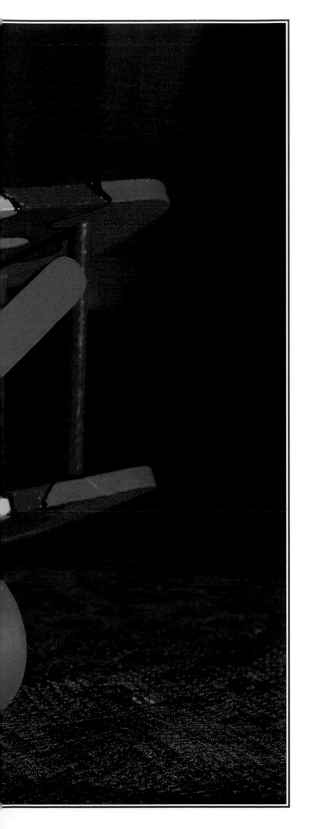

SOPWITH CAMEL

BIPLANE

Since the components of this Sopwith Camel must slot together, it presents more of a challenge than some of the toys already featured.

The fuselage is shaped from a solid block of wood, which is tapered towards the back. The lower wings are recessed into the fuselage, and are then held in position by the two undercarriage struts. The upper wing is fixed to the lower wing by four short dowels, and the tailplane is anchored to the fuselage by the skid, which is an extension of the tail.

This is not a difficult toy to make, but if you have a router which can be mounted in a drill stand or a router bench, the morticing, and the recessing and slotting of the wings, becomes very much easier. *(For advice on using a router see pages 131-3.)*

MATERIALS

1⅜in x 1¾in x 9in (35mm x 45mm x 230mm) pine or hardwood
2in x 1in (50mm x 25mm) pine or hardwood
¼in (6mm) birch-faced plywood offcuts
³⁄₁₆in (4mm) dowel
¼in (6mm) dowel
½in (12mm) dowel

TOOLS

Pillar drill, jigsaw, router, lathe

1 Cut out all of the plywood components except for the rear wing. Plane the edges and round the corners, then drill the holes for the axle and propeller shaft. Mark on the top surface of each front wing the position of the struts. The holes are in exactly the same position in both wings, but it is not easy to stack them and drill them together. Once you have marked the location of the four holes, make a very simple angled ramp and clamp it to the bed of the pillar drill.

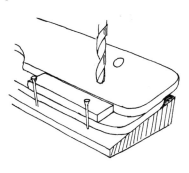

2 Mark out the rear wing at right angles to the side of the sheet of plywood. Cut out the slot for the tailplane with the router, controlling the tool by setting the fence against the side of the plywood sheet. Now cut out the wing and round and smooth its edges.

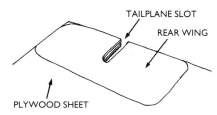

TAILPLANE SLOT

REAR WING

PLYWOOD SHEET

3 Plane the fuselage block to size, but do not cut it to length because a little extra length will help to control the router. Mark in the ends, the recesses for the lower and rear wings, the slot for the tailplane and the mortices for the undercarriage. Drill the holes for the airman and his machine-gun with the pillar drill.

Cut out the slot for the tailplane and undercarriage struts first. Use the router fence to limit sideways movement of the cutter, and the plunge facility and depth stop to make the slots.

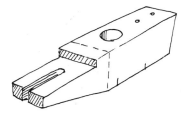

4 Next saw across the marks which define the ends of the wing slots, taking care to keep to the waste side of the lines. Remove the router fence, set the depth stop to ¼in (6mm), check it on some waste wood and then remove the waste inside the marks in easy stages, but not more than ¹⁄₂in (1mm) at a time.

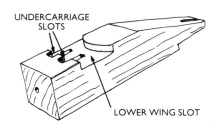

UNDERCARRIAGE SLOTS

LOWER WING SLOT

5 Fit the lower front wing. If it does not fit, use a sharp chisel to trim back the leading edge of the slot until it slips tightly into position. Press the undercarriage struts into their slots immediately in front of the wing to hold it in position. Similarly fit the tailplane, which holds the rear wing in place. Its lower point should form the skid.

Cut the fuselage to length. Drill the hole in the front for the propeller shaft with a ¼in (6mm) metalworking drill. Taper the sides of the fuselage with a chisel and plane them smooth.

6 Once all the parts are sanded, smooth, glue and pin the rear wing and lower front wing, and glue the tailplane in place.

Cut four ¼in (6mm) dowel struts to length with a penknife as described on page 14. Fit the struts into the holes in the lower wing, and glue them with clear, cellulose-based modelling cement. The advantage of this glue is that, unlike PVA glue, it will not swell the dowels and prevent accurate adjustment.

When the glue has hardened, trim the ends of the struts with a chisel and smooth the wings with 220-grit sandpaper.

Fit the wheels, propeller and engine cowling. If you do not have a lathe, carve a rectangular radiator, making the model resemble a Bristol F2B rather than a Sopwith Camel SE.

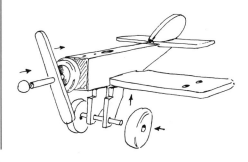

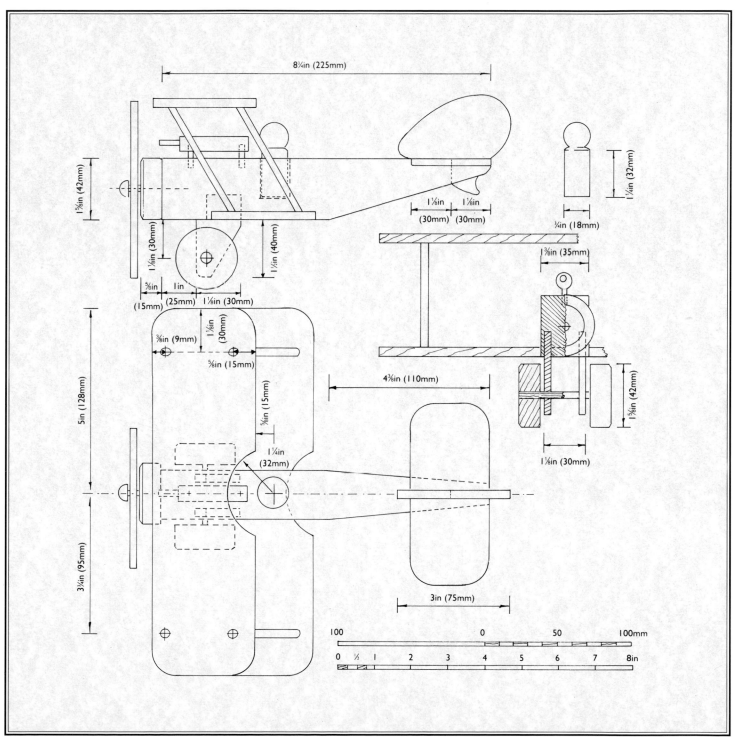

8¼in (225mm)

1⅝in (42mm)

1⅛in (30mm)

1½in (40mm)

⅝in (15mm)

1in (25mm)

1⅛in (30mm)

1⅛in (30mm)

1⅛in (30mm)

¾in (18mm)

1⅜in (35mm)

1¼in (32mm)

1⅝in (42mm)

1⅛in (30mm)

4⅜in (110mm)

⅜in (9mm)

1⅛in (30mm)

⅝in (15mm)

⅝in (15mm)

5in (128mm)

1¼in (32mm)

3¾in (95mm)

3in (75mm)

100   0   50   100mm

0 ½ 1   2   3   4   5   6   7   8in

ACTION
TOYS

FIRE ENGINE

Blocks and slabs of wood are glued together to make this model of a 1922 Ahrens-Fox R-K-4 Pumper fire engine. It is equipped with a hose which can be wound in by turning the crank on the running board and an extending ladder hangs on the rear handrails. Three wooden firemen, turned from ¾in (18mm) dowel, stand on the platform at the rear of the engine, and two more sit next to the driver. The bench seat, held by a single screw driven up between the chassis members, can be removed to facilitate painting this toy.

MATERIALS

¾in x 4in (18mm x 100mm) pine
3in x 2½in (75mm x 65mm) pine
3in x 1½in (75mm x 40mm) pine
¼in (6mm) plywood
³⁄₁₆in (4mm) dowel
¼in (6mm) dowel
½in (12mm) dowel
¾in (18mm) dowel
MDF (medium-density fibreboard)
  offcut

TOOLS

Pillar drill, lathe, jigsaw

1 Cut all of the components to shape before assembling the fire engine in the following order.

2 Shape and drill the chassis for the axles, hose crank and pinion. Drill and fit plywood plate 1.

Shape the engine block and the radiator.

Rout or carve the recess for the radiator grill. The easiest way to do this is to trace round the radiator grill on an offcut of MDF. Then draw on the MDF the inner line which marks the edge of the grill. Cut along this line with a fretsaw, and smooth the sawcut with a file. Tack the radiator onto the MDF. Fit a small-diameter cutter in the router and mount it in the router stand. Set the depth stop to $\frac{1}{16}$in (2mm) and with the guide pin locating against the inside of the template, lower the cutter, and rout out the recess for the sandpaper grill. *(For advice on routing see pages 131-3.)*

Pin and glue the radiator to the engine block and glue the engine in position. Glue the radiator grill in position.

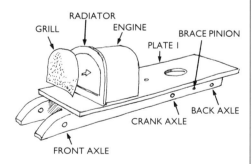

3 Fit the rear platform support and glue it in place.

Drill the holes in plate 3 and saw out the hose hatch.

Glue plates 2 and 3 to plate 1. Fit the dashboard and footrest.

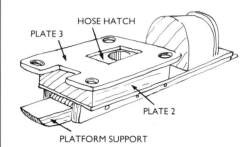

4 Fit, drill and glue the rear platform to its support, holding it in alignment temporarily with two $\frac{1}{2}$in (12mm) dowels.

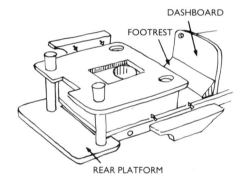

5 Glue tapered strips to the chassis sides and plate 2. Fit the running boards. Fit the steering wheel and column.

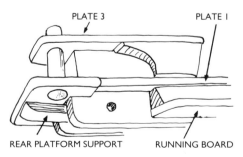

6 Make up the bench seat and screw it in place temporarily.

7 Glue the reel brackets, water cylinder, tool boxes, steps, radiator cap, horn and bell.

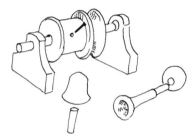

8 Fit the pressure cylinder and faucets but do not glue them until they have been painted.

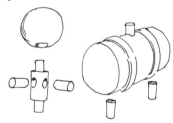

9 Turn, drill and fit the vertical posts and handrails. *(For advice on turning see pages 133-8.)* Glue them in position with cellulose-based modelling cement.

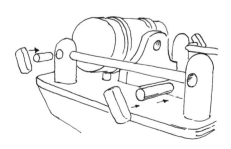

10 Assemble the hose crank, pulley and wire brace. Insert the pulley between the chassis members, and poke the crank axle through the chassis into the reel. Align the holes in the reel and axle, and press a pin through the two to lock them together.

The wire brace guides the thread from the pulley onto the narrow spool at the forward end of the hose reel. When the hose is unwound, the thread is pulled from the pulley and winds onto the spool. The hose can be wound in by turning the small crank fitted at the end of the crank axle. Make the brace from small-diameter copper or galvanized wire, and hold it in position with the brace pinion. Adjust the position of the brace with a pair of long-nosed pliers then lock the pinion in position by spotting a little cellulose-based modelling cement over the ends of the holes in the chassis.

When the fire engine is completely painted, dismantle the hose reel and nail the end of the braided cord, which is the hose, to the reel. Next, poke the end of the winding thread through the hole in the spool, and tie it to stop it pulling out. Wind the hose onto the reel, and make a few turns round the spool with the thread. Fit the reel back into position, and feed the thread through the brace, under the pinion, and through the thread hole in the pulley. Pull the hose off the reel. This will wind more thread onto the spool. Now fasten the other end of the thread to the pulley.

The nozzle is made from a short length of ¼in (6mm) dowel, carved to the shape with a penknife. The end of the hose is cemented into a hole bored in the end of the nozzle, and the bent veneer pin is pressed through the side of the nozzle into the hose to secure it.

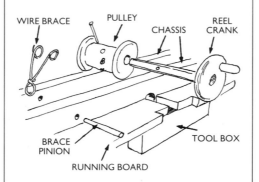

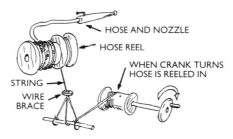

11 Finish painting all of the components before glueing them in position, and fit the wheels after the paint has dried thoroughly.

MAKING LADDERS

12 The ladder rungs in the model shown here are made from 1½in (40mm) wire nails with their heads snipped off. Wooden toothpicks or bamboo barbecue skewers will do just as well, and are easier to cut.

All four ladder sides can be drilled at the same time. Choose a suitably large strip of straight-grained, square-section pine of ½in x 1in x 7in (12mm x 25mm x 175mm) and mark along one edge the position for each rung. Select a suitable drill for the rungs. Check that the rungs make a tight press fit in a sample drill hole before drilling holes for all the rungs.

13 Set the drill bit in the pillar drill and, without switching it on, lower and hold the point of the bit on the centrepoint of one of the middle rung holes. Clamp or tack a fence hard against the back of the ladder strip to ensure that each rung is set the same distance from the edge of the ladder. Now drill each rung hole, pressing the drill right through the strip.

14 All that remains to be done is to slice the strip into four with the circular saw. Plane and smooth each strip and assemble each section of the ladder, using cellulose-based modelling cement. The hooks on the top section of the ladder are made from bent veneer pins. The lower brace is either cross-halved in wood, or can be made from a small strip of tin, bent and fixed with a pin as illustrated.

Fill the cavities at the rung ends with a two-part wood filler.

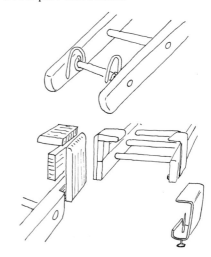

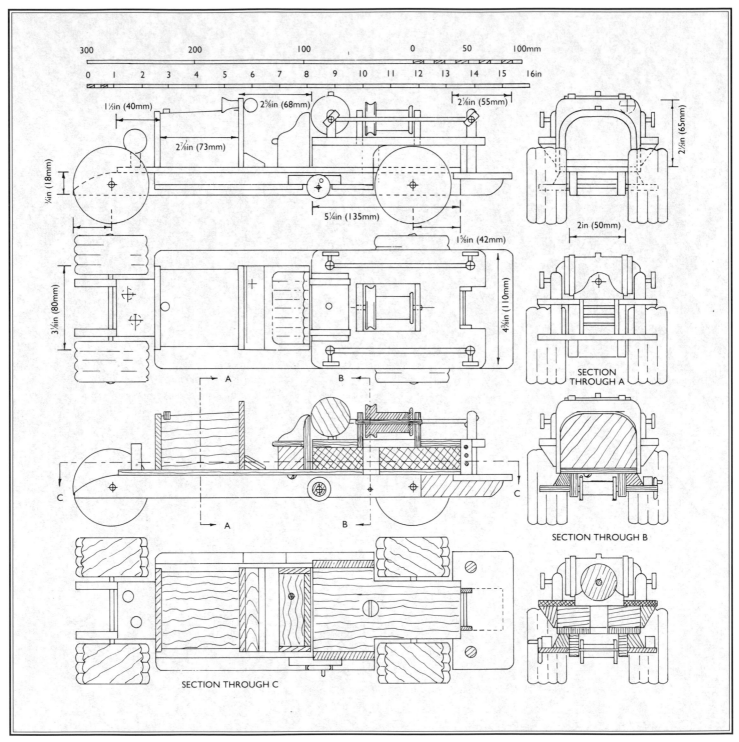

AXLES

Most of the smaller carpet toys can be fitted with either ¼in (6mm) dowel axles *(see page 14)*, or with steel rod axles. Dowels are not as strong, yet they seem to last very well. Suitable steel rods are not readily available, but for most of these toys, 6in (150mm) wire nails will be long enough and strong enough.

CUTTING DOWELS
It is not necessary to saw a dowel unless it is more than ⅜in (9mm) thick. Instead, mark on it the length you require and then, using a sharp penknife, roll the dowel with the blade of the knife, pressing down firmly. Snap the dowel when you have incised its outer fibres. This gives a cleaner and swifter cut than sawing.

FITTING STEEL AXLES
This is the last job to do, after all the paint is dry. Unless you are very concerned about appearances, retain the flat top to the nail on one side of the vehicle. The other end will have to be swaged to prevent the opposite wheel from rolling off. To do this, measure the axle length, add about ¹⁄₁₆in (2mm) beyond the outer washer for the swaging, then saw off the point of the nail. Slip the wheels and washers on the axle, and rest the vehicle on its side with the axle centred on a block of heavy scrap iron. Fit the last washer over the end of the nail. This should be

a particularly tight-fitting washer, otherwise it will jump off when you start burring the edge of the axle.

Carry on hitting the edge of the axle outwards using light blows with the back of the hammer, until you have formed a mushroom-shaped end which holds the washer and the wheels in position.

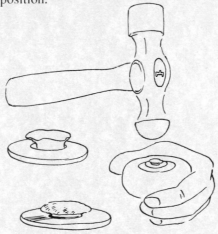

Problems arise if the washer is too large, and repeatedly jumps off. The only thing you can do, if a smaller washer is not available, is remove the axle and start the swaging in the vice, checking now and again that it will still fit through the wheels and chassis, or swage the inside edge of the washer with a hammer and punch to reduce its diameter. When you have started the swage, reassemble the components and continue as before, tapping and gently rounding and burring the edge of the sawn axle.

SECURING WHEELS
The system of rivetting allows the wheels to turn freely on the metal axle. Sometimes it is necessary to attach the wheel to the axle so that the wheel rotates with the axle (see Steam Train on page 107). There are two simple ways to ensure a firm bond between the axle and the wheel: glueing the wheel to the axle and pinning it.

Sandpaper the ends of the axle to remove any grease. Support the axle on an iron block and punch its sides with a centrepunch. This raises a sharp lip at the edges of the punchmark, which will give the glue a good hold. Mix some epoxy resin. Dip the ends of the axles into the glue, and then poke the end of the axle into the wheel. Drop more glue into the wheel hole, before covering the hole with a scrap of leather or plastic, and then hammering the axle into position. The glue captured inside the wheel will harden the wood fibres which press against the axle, and prevent the wheel working loose.

Alternatively, saw a slot in each end of the axle. Press the axle into the wheel, and then, when both wheels are in position, drive a panel pin diagonally into the wheel. Start the pin in the slot, and tap it sideways into the wheel. The pin wedges the axle apart, and as the head nears the slot, turn the vehicle on its side and tap the pin head sideways into the slot, widening it more.

MOBILE STEAM CRANE

Two winches mounted in the cab wind in the hook and raise and lower the jib. The crane's body can be rotated by turning a wheel mounted on the cabin. At the back of the cabin there is a boiler, separated by a steel railing from the winches, wires, ratchets and pawls in the open front. The main winch turns the flywheel and drives the powerful cylinder. Both winches operate through pulleys, so this crane has considerable lifting power, particularly when the jib is at maximum elevation.

The roof covering the cabin is fastened with two screws, allowing it to be removed so that the ropes and winches can be serviced. The curved roof is made from seven strips of pine glued together. *(For guidance on turning wheels and pulleys see pages 134-6.)*

This crane will take several days to build because many small detailed components must be made. Because of the large number of moving parts mounted in the cabin walls, it is necessary to exercise a tight dimensional control during its initial setting out and assembly

Make the crane in the order listed below. Page references for relevant skills are given in brackets.

MATERIALS

1½in x 1½in (40mm x 40mm) pine
2in x 1½in (50mm x 40mm) pine
¾in x 4in (18mm x 100mm) pine
¼in (6mm) birch-faced plywood
³⁄₁₆in (4mm) MDF (offcuts)
¼in (6mm) dowel
1½in x ¼in (40mm x 6mm) coach
  bolt

TOOLS

Lathe, pillar drill, jigsaw

1 Cut out all of the main components. Drill the holes in the cabin sides with the two sides tacked together. Turn the two 4in (100mm) bearing rings. Mark the centrepoints for the ¼in (6mm) diameter holes around the perimeter of one, then stack the two rings together and drill them with the pillar drill. Cut out the centre disc of the top ring on the lathe *(see page 136)*.

2 Fit the centre block between the chassis members, and nail and glue the chassis together.

Cut and glue the 14 short dowels *(see page 14)* to complete the bearing ring. Nail and glue the ring to the chassis.

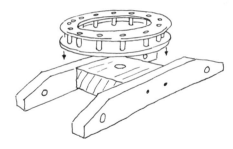

3 Assemble the jib mounting bracket and nail and glue it to the crane base. Glue the centre disc to the underside of the crane base. The sloping edge of the centre disc should fit against the inside rim of the bearing ring, and limits sideways movement between the base and the chassis.

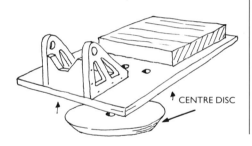

CENTRE DISC

4 Nail and glue the cabin floor to the crane base.

Glue on the back of the cabin, then the sides. Fit the front roof beam into the notches in the sides of the cabin.

Fit the base for the boiler. Plane the top edges of the cabin so they meet flush with the curved roof beams.

Fit the boiler and the railing *(see pages 63-4)*. The door can also be cut out and hinged to the doorpost, and the assembly glued into the doorway at the back of the cabin *(see page 45)*. Line the window with four thin lining strips *(see pages 61-2)*.

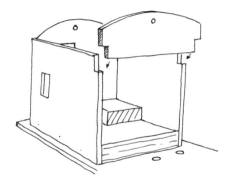

5 Cut out two extra roof beams and screw them against the ends of the cabin, on the inside. Make up the curved top, glueing the strips against each other and onto the extra roof beams screwed

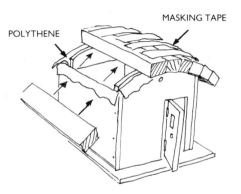

MASKING TAPE

POLYTHENE

to the ends of the cabin. When the glue is dry, remove the roof by unscrewing the two screws at the ends of the cabin.

6 Smooth the top and trim the ends square with a block plane before cutting the hole in the top for the jib control rope. Square the hole with a ⅜in (9mm) chisel, then fit the pre-assembled rope guide.

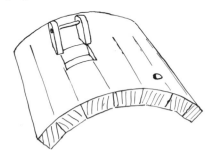

7 Drill through the cabin and boiler to accommodate the cylinder pivot bolt. Glue the cylinder spacer block to the side of the cabin and clamp it temporarily with the cylinder pivot bolt.

8 Cut the piston arm from ¼in (6mm) dowel, saw a 'v' in the end with the fretsaw *(see pages 127-8)*. Cut out and drill the end bearing, and trim the extension on it to fit into the 'v' slot in the piston arm and then glue the two pieces together.

PIVOT BOLT   SPACER BLOCK

MOUNTING BLOCK

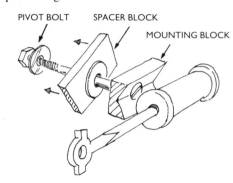

9 Assemble the winches. Drill through the winch barrels into the axles using a veneer or panel pin as the drill bit. (It may be necessary to wrap a couple of turns of masking tape around the end of the pin to improve its grip in the drill chuck.)

Fit and adjust the pawls.

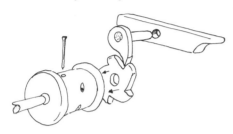

10 Assemble the cylinder with the head of the pivot bolt trapped beside the cylinder and held by the cylinder mounting block. Glue the mounting block to the cylinder.

Fit the flywheel to the end of the axle of the main winch and feed the piston arm up into the cylinder. Slip a washer over the pivot bolt and press the bolt through the side of the cabin and through the boiler. Screw on the securing nut. When the main winch is turned, the piston should slide up and down inside the cylinder. If it does not, try slackening the pivot bolt nut. If this does not work, and you are certain that the piston arm is not too long and is jamming inside the cylinder at the top of the stroke, ream out the cylinder bore and the hole in the end bearing, using a slightly larger drill bit.

11 Cut the jib to length, and drill the pivot hole at its base. Hold the jib in the vice and plane the taper with a smoothing plane. Work the sides in pairs, trying to keep adjacent sides at right angles. When all four sides are tapered, and both end sections are square, mark off and plane the corners. If you hold the plane at 45 degrees to the square sides, making three cuts per corner before turning the jib round, it will be easy to keep the taper regular.

12 Mark off on the top end of the jib the location of the two plywood cheeks which hold the top pulley. Cut out the two recesses and glue the cheeks to the jib. Shape them as illustrated and then drill the pivot hole.

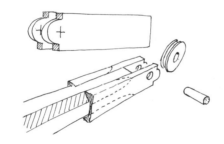

13 Cut and fit the crane turning cog and the ¼in (6mm) wooden axle. Join the crane to its base, using small spacer blocks and steel washers to lift the crane base slightly above the top of the bearing ring, to minimize friction. Drill the hole in the overhanging cabin roof for the axle and fit the large-diameter turning crank to its top. When you operate the turning crank the tips of the cog should press against the rungs of the bearing ring, and rotate the body of the crane.

Fit the water tank and the plywood anchorage points on the jib and the roof.

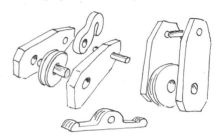

14 Make the pulley blocks. Dismantle the crane before painting it. Run the electric drill, fitted with an appropriate bit, through each axle and hole before beginning the final assembly.

(For instructions on fitting axles see page 33; for using a fretsaw see pages 127-8, for making railings see pages 63-4; and for turning wheels and ratchets see pages 134-6.)

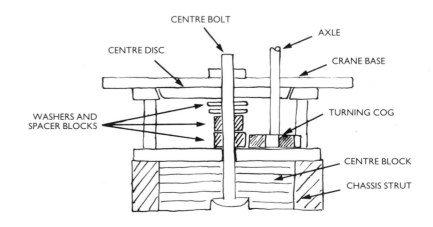

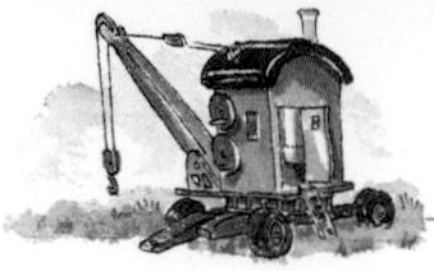

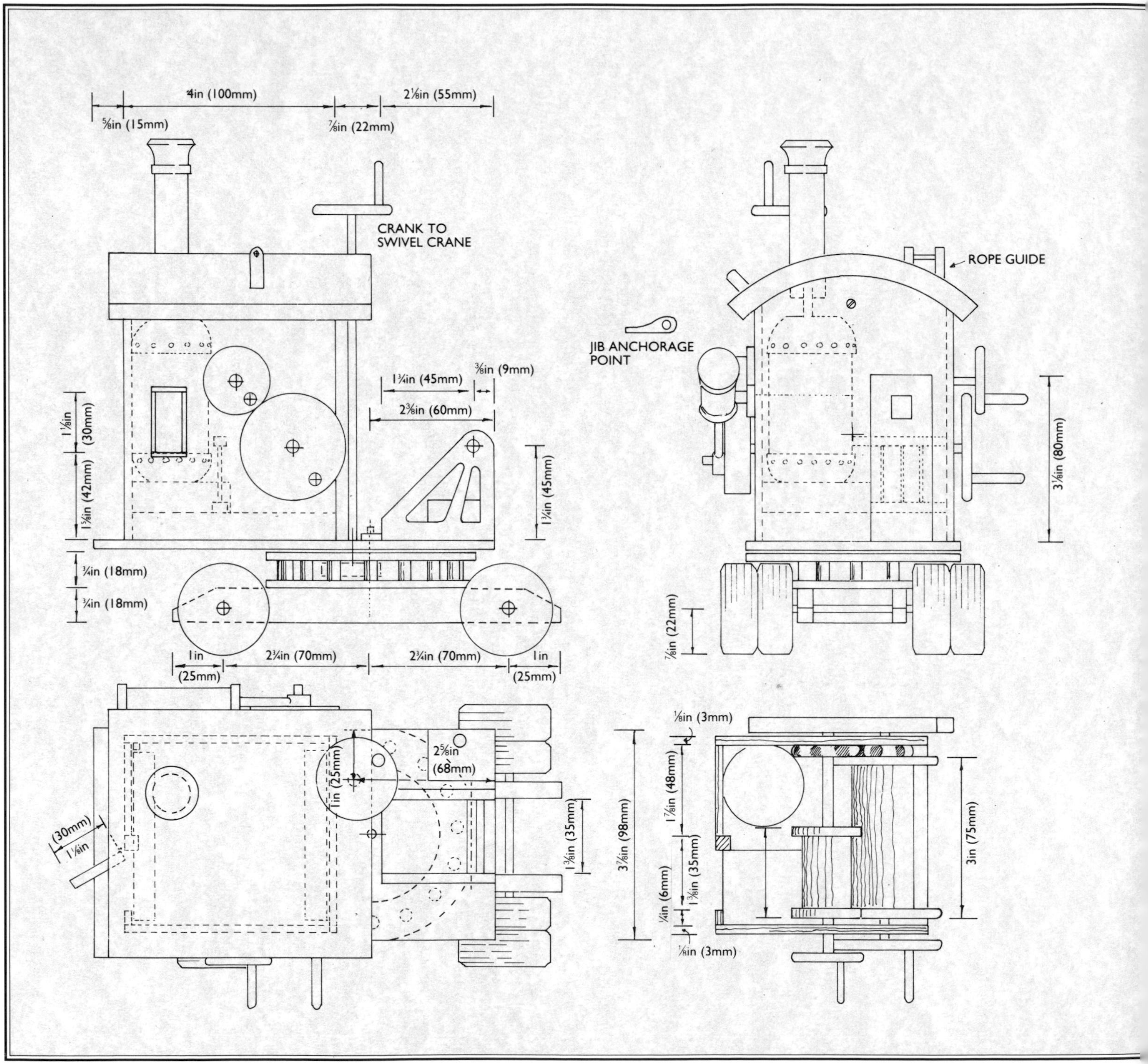
4in (100mm)
2 1/8in (55mm)
5/8in (15mm)
7/8in (22mm)
CRANK TO SWIVEL CRANE
ROPE GUIDE
JIB ANCHORAGE POINT
1 3/4in (45mm)
3/8in (9mm)
2 3/8in (60mm)
1 1/8in (30mm)
1 5/8in (42mm)
1 3/4in (45mm)
3/4in (18mm)
3/4in (18mm)
3 1/8in (80mm)
7/8in (22mm)
1in (25mm)
2 3/4in (70mm)
2 3/4in (70mm)
1in (25mm)
2 5/8in (68mm)
1in (25mm)
(30mm) 1 1/8in
1 3/8in (35mm)
3 7/8in (98mm)
1/8in (3mm)
1 7/8in (48mm)
1 3/8in (35mm)
1/4in (6mm)
1/8in (3mm)
3in (75mm)

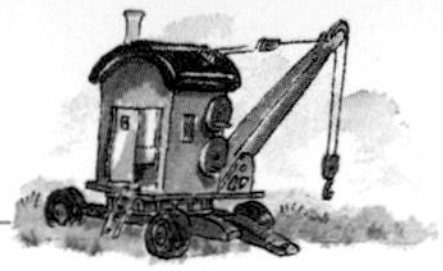

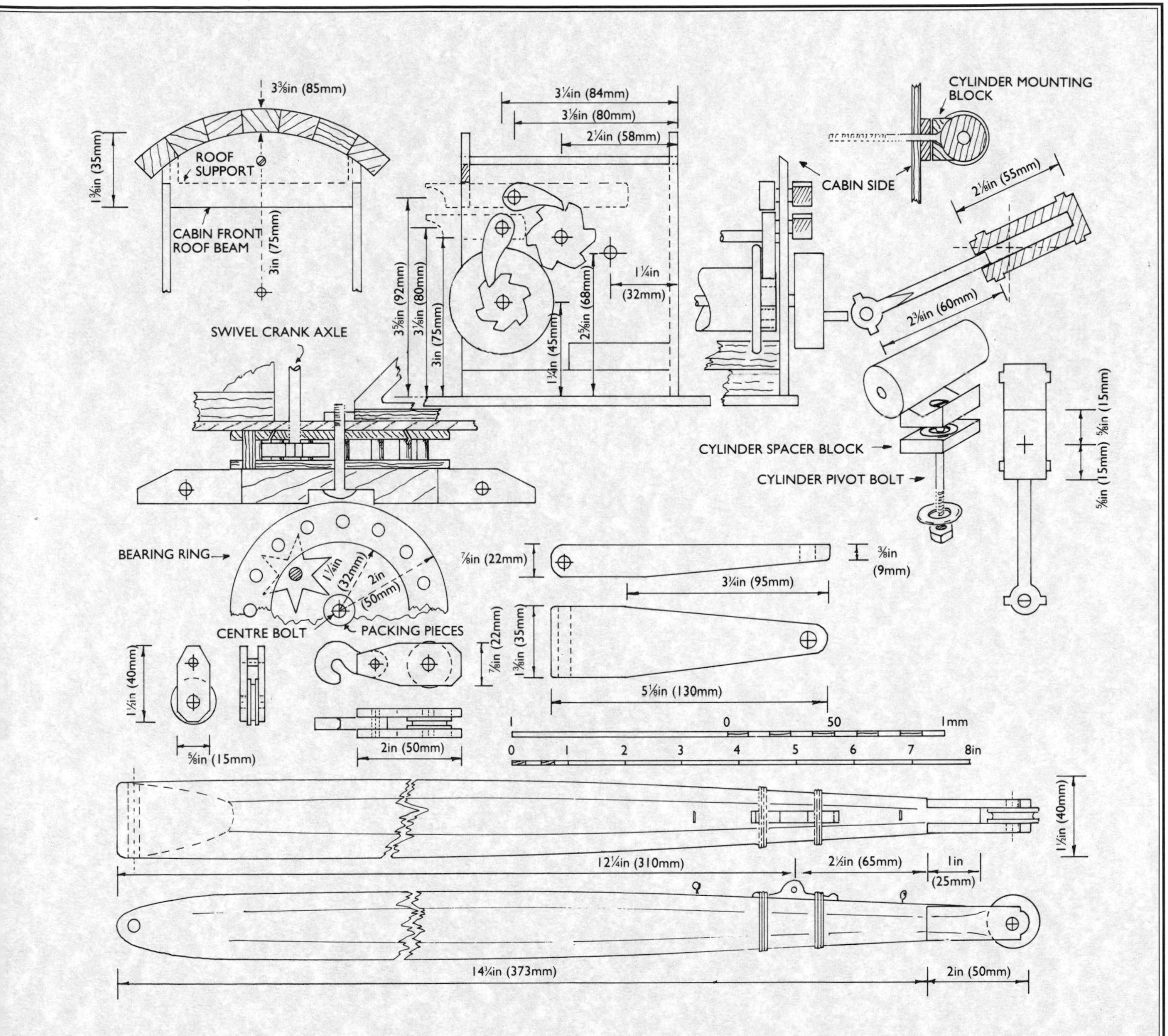
3⅜in (85mm)
1⅜in (35mm)
ROOF SUPPORT
CABIN FRONT ROOF BEAM
3in (75mm)
3¼in (84mm)
3⅛in (80mm)
2¼in (58mm)
3⅝in (92mm)
3⅛in (80mm)
3in (75mm)
1¾in (45mm)
2⅝in (68mm)
1¼in (32mm)
CYLINDER MOUNTING BLOCK
CABIN SIDE
2⅛in (55mm)
2⅜in (60mm)
SWIVEL CRANK AXLE
CYLINDER SPACER BLOCK
CYLINDER PIVOT BOLT
⅝in (15mm)
⅝in (15mm)
BEARING RING
1¼in (32mm)
2in (50mm)
CENTRE BOLT
PACKING PIECES
⅞in (22mm)
⅜in (9mm)
3¾in (95mm)
1⅜in (35mm)
⅞in (22mm)
5⅛in (130mm)
1½in (40mm)
⅝in (15mm)
2in (50mm)
0
50
1mm
0
1
2
3
4
5
6
7
8in
1½in (40mm)
12¼in (310mm)
2½in (65mm)
1in (25mm)
14¾in (373mm)
2in (50mm)

BUILDINGS

TRADITIONAL BARN

This traditional American barn has three rooms on the ground floor and a hayloft above. Two double doors give access to the hayloft and the large store below it. At the back of the barn there is a storeroom and a stable. A trapdoor leads from the stable to the hayloft.

Although this is a simple toy, it incorporates a number of attractive features. The loft space is beamed and raftered and there are beams on the walls and ceiling of the lower floor. A doorway linking the two stores provides intriguing views, adding to this toy's magic.

Note that the plans show mitred wall joints. This simple method of jointing is very easy to achieve. However, if you prefer to butt-join the corners, subtract ¼in (6mm) from each side of the end panels.

MATERIALS

¼in (6mm) MDF or birch-faced
  plywood
³⁄₁₆in (4mm) MDF or birch-faced
  plywood
½in x 4in (12mm x 100mm) pine
  strip
1½in (40mm) brass hinge
8 x ½in (12mm) doll's house hinges

TOOLS

Fretsaw or jigsaw, router and stand

1 Cut out the sides, base, floor and partition boards. Trim them with a plane, holding together with pins pieces of the same size, to ensure that they are cut to the same dimension. Mark and cut out the doorways and windows, leaving space for the window lining strips and for the doorposts which support the two small doors at the back of the barn.

2 Set up the router in the router stand, and fit a mitre bit. Set a fence as explained on page 133, so that the router slices off a 45-degree cut in a single pass. If you are using a thin scrap of waste wood for a fence, tack it down to the router stand to prevent the sharp edge of the newly formed mitre sliding beneath it.

Check that the router is set up correctly by testing it on a piece of scrap wood. Then cut the end mitres in turn, passing the workpiece from left to right, making sure that it is pressed firmly against the fence.

3 Once the mitres are cut, lay out the sides in their correct order, inside face downwards on the workbench, and with the bottom of each piece lined against a straight batten. Tape the mitres together with masking tape. Turn the whole assembly over and pull the two ends together, holding them temporarily with tape. Insert the upper floor to keep the sides square.

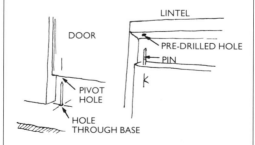

MASKING TAPE

4 After checking that all the parts fit together, remove the strip of tape holding the ends together, lay out the taped-together row of sides and ends, and run glue down each open mitre. Fold the sides together and tape up the last mitre to close the structure. Insert the floor to hold it all square.

Mark on the base the exact outline of the inside of the barn, and glue small temporary blocks against the line to locate the sides.

5 Now that the glue holding the mitres is dry, remove the masking tape and place the sides over the blocks. Pencil in the pivot points for the doors at the end of the large store. Each door pivots on two pins. One pin pokes up through the floor of the barn into the bottom of the door while the other pin, vertically above the first, is driven into the top of the door and locates in a hole in the underside of the lintel.

```
                              LINTEL

       DOOR                        PRE-DRILLED HOLE
                                   PIN



                    PIVOT
                    HOLE

                    HOLE
                    THROUGH BASE
```

6 Once the holes for the main doors have been drilled, the sides can be

glued to the base and the partition walls fitted. Drill and fit the lintel. Cut and fit all the vertical beams around the sides of the three rooms, making sure that none of the beams extends beyond the height of the partitions.

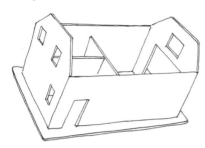

7 Provided that the beams are not too long, they do not need to be fitted accurately, since the horizontal joists which are glued beneath the loft floor will hide any gaps.

8 When the decorative work on the ground floor walls is finished, the loft floor can be fitted, followed by the

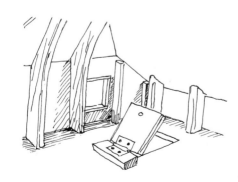

trapdoor, and then more short beams on the side and end walls. Glue and fit the angled knees and the sloping roofs supported by them at the ends of the barn.

9 The barn is now ready for the finishing work. Fit the doors and window strips, along with any other features that you may want to add, such as hoists and ladders. Then fit and adjust the four main roof panels, holding them temporarily with tape to check their fit. When they are ready, glue the two lower roofs each side of the barn. Add the inner applied framework and then glue on an upper pitch and fit more framework inside.

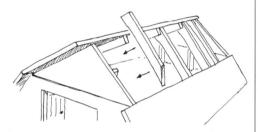

10 Finally glue the remaining rafters inside the barn, to connect the ridge with the lower pitch on the last side, before glueing the last section of roof in place. It is not necessary to paint the inside of the loft.

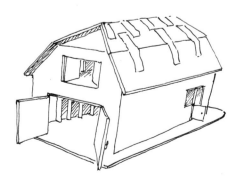

APPLIED BEAMS AND RAFTERS

11 Any straight-grained pine strip will do to simulate heavy beams. The strips need to be about ¼in (6mm) thick and about ⅝in (15mm) wide and can be left rough-sawn. Chamfer the exposed corners with a chisel or penknife. Use a glue gun or contact adhesive.

DOORS

12 The illustrations below show the detail of the three different styles of door hanging used in this barn. (The hinges for the store door, trapdoor and upper double doors are fitted before the door jambs are installed.)

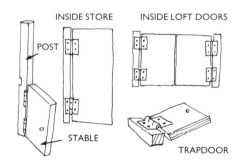

INSIDE STORE   INSIDE LOFT DOORS

POST

STABLE

TRAPDOOR

13 There should be a slight gap between the door jamb and the door, and inserting a temporary strip of thin card between them will help ensure accurate alignment while the hinge is

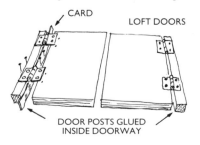

CARD

LOFT DOORS

DOOR POSTS GLUED INSIDE DOORWAY

nailed in position.

14 Because the grain of the pine door jamb is likely to deflect the nail holding the hinge, it is best to mark and then start the nail holes with a veneer pin before nailing the hinges in place with brass nails.

The main doors are first fitted into the doorway, and then the edges against the door frame are radiused with a block plane. Pencil the location of the pivot hole in the lintel onto the front face of the lintel. Place the door in position and transfer the mark to the top of the door.

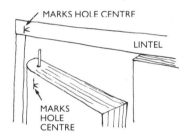

MARKS HOLE CENTRE

LINTEL

MARKS HOLE CENTRE

15 Now tap a veneer pin into the top of the door as illustrated, and cut it off ³⁄₁₆in (4mm) above the door. Replace the door, sliding the pin into the hole in the lintel. Hold the door in position, and press a veneer pin into the hole in the base of the barn and into the wood at the bottom of the door, before giving the pin a light tap with a hammer.

16 If the door does not open easily, you may have to adjust the radius at the door frame, if that is jamming, or reposition the lower pin. To do the latter, pack thin card between the door and the frame to ensure that the pin makes a new hole and does not slide into the existing hole at the second attempt to find the right pivot point.

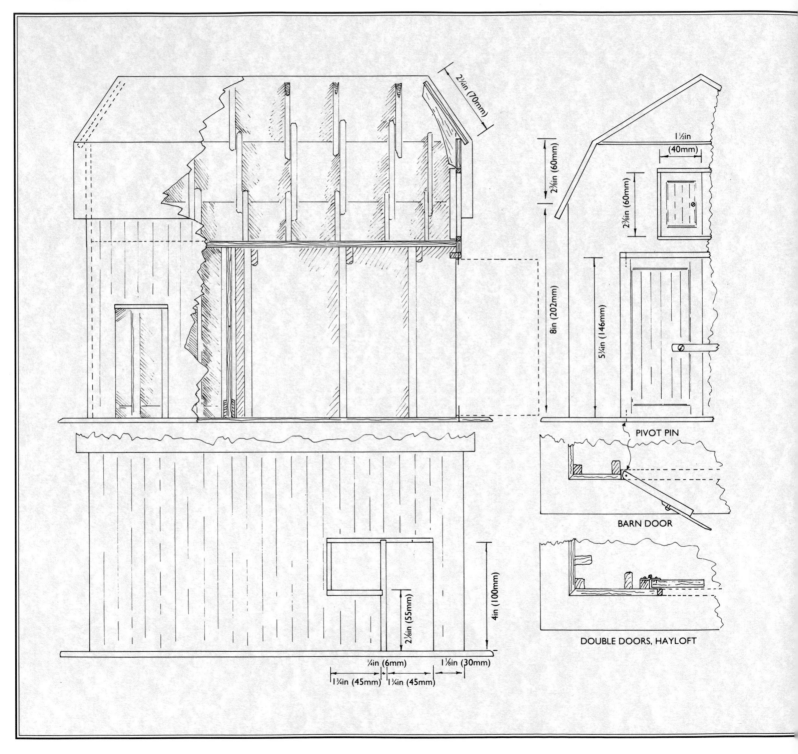

2¾in (70mm)

1½in (40mm)

2⅜in (60mm)

2⅜in (60mm)

8in (202mm)

5¾in (146mm)

PIVOT PIN

BARN DOOR

4in (100mm)

2⅛in (55mm)

DOUBLE DOORS, HAYLOFT

¼in (6mm)

1⅛in (30mm)

1¾in (45mm)   1¾in (45mm)

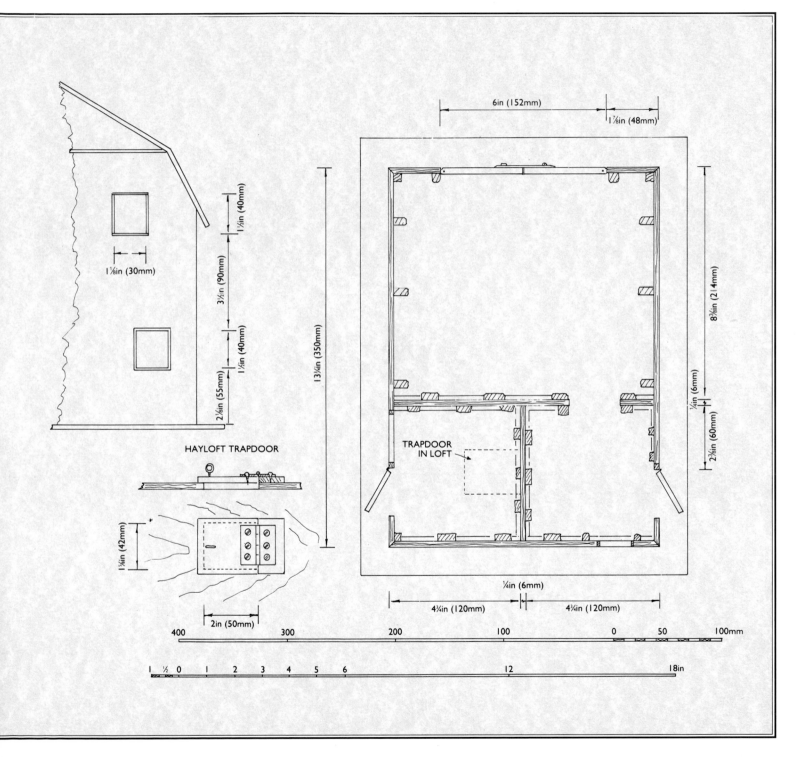

1⅛in (30mm)

1½in (40mm)

3½in (90mm)

1½in (40mm)

2⅛in (55mm)

13¾in (350mm)

HAYLOFT TRAPDOOR

1⅝in (42mm)

2in (50mm)

6in (152mm)

1⅞in (48mm)

8⅜in (214mm)

¼in (6mm)

2⅜in (60mm)

TRAPDOOR
IN LOFT

¼in (6mm)

4¾in (120mm)

4¾in (120mm)

400   300   200   100   0   50   100mm

1 ½ 0 1 2 3 4 5 6   12   18in

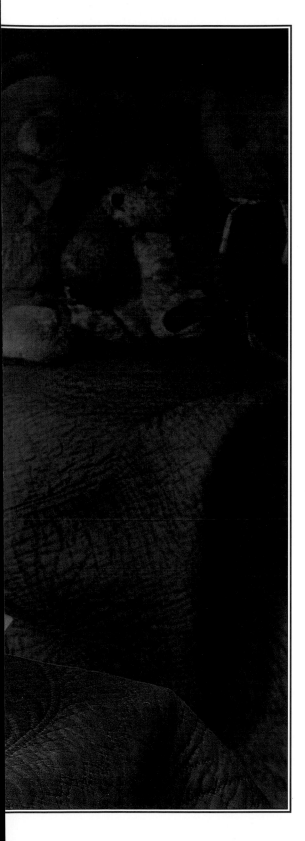

MOATED CASTLE

This castle is built in three separate parts: the dungeons, the main outer walls and towers and the keep. After the painting is completed, the keep and the main courtyard are glued together. A door high in the back of the keep gives access to the accommodation there.

The dungeons remain separate, but are held to the main structure by a simple catch which is operated at the back of the castle. Soldiers, knights and horses can be stored there. Access to the dungeons, when the castle is fitted together, is via the oubliette, which is inside the main gate and down the steps beside the keep. A punt on a long line carries supplies into the dungeons, and bodies out.

This toy is designed to be built with the very minimum of handwork. All of the components are shaped by the router. This enables you to add details such as extra crenellations, windows, arrow slits, towers and so on. If you want to add your own features, it is a good idea to include windows, gratings and doors to illuminate the gloomy corners.

MATERIALS

³⁄₁₆in (4mm) MDF
¼in (6mm) MDF
2in x 1½in (50mm x 40mm) pine
2in x 4in (50mm x 100mm) pine
½in x ½in (12mm x 12mm) pine or
   quadrant moulding
¼in (6mm) dowel
1½in (40mm) cranked hinge

TOOLS

Jigsaw, drill stand and router with
⅛in/3.2mm straight cutter and
½in/12.7mm, 45-degree 'v' groove
cutter

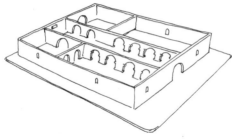

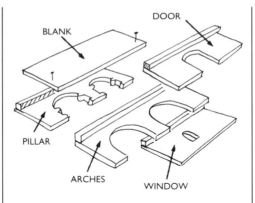

BASE

1 All of the techniques for making this toy are described elsewhere in this book. The order of construction is given below, as well as some suggestions for making very simple routing templates.

Cut out the base and the 1½in (40mm) wide strips for the dungeon walls from ¼in (6mm) MDF. Make templates for cutting out the arches, doors, pillars and windows for the dungeons.

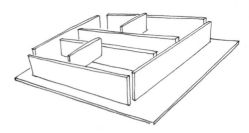

2 Cut the corner mitre joints, using the mitre cutter set in the router, and pressing the jointing edge against the fence, as illustrated. *(For advice on mitre cutting see page 133.)*

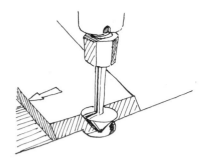

3 Cut the interior walls to length. Rout out the catch slot, doorways and pillars in the dungeon walls.

Mark the wall plan on the castle base and drive pins into the base to locate the sides and inner walls.

4 Construct the simple catch shown in the plans.

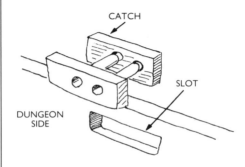

5 Glue the outer walls together *(see page 44)*. Glue the bottom of the outer walls and lower them onto the base, locating them in position with the pins driven into the base.

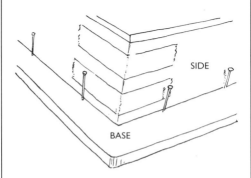

6 Glue the inner walls to the base and the side walls.

7 Drill holes for the iron gratings and glue them in position. Clamp the top of the gratings with a wooden brace which is glued to the top edge of the wall as illustrated.

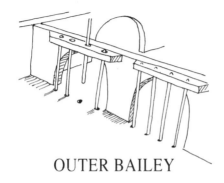

OUTER BAILEY

8 Cut out the base of the outer bailey and chamfer its edge. Rout or fretsaw out the oubliettes, grills, stairwells, garderobes etc.

Cut out a 48in x 4in (1.13m x 100mm) strip of ¼in (6mm) MDF for the four exterior walls. Cut the walls to length (12in/305mm), making sure the ends are sawn square to the base of the wall.

Rout out the crenellations and the windows. Rout out all the doo. including the main entrance.

Cut a 39in x 1¾in (1m x 45mm) strip for the inner walkway. Cut a 27½in x ¾in (700mm x 18mm) strip for the parapet.

Rout the 45-degree mitres each wall's inside edge *(see pages 131-3)*.

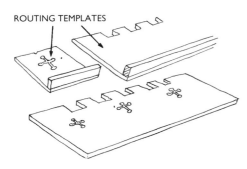

ROUTING TEMPLATES

9 Mark and saw the 45-degree mitres on the ends of the inner walkway. The mitres at the corners of the walkways do not need to be accurate, provided that the combined angles at any corner do not exceed 90 degrees. Errors will be concealed by a corner block and tower once the walls are erected.

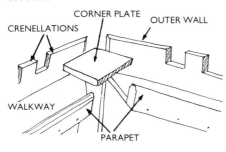

CRENELLATIONS CORNER PLATE OUTER WALL
WALKWAY
PARAPET

10 Glue and pin the walkways to the inside of the two side walls and front walls. Two nails, or a simple fence nailed to the workbench close to the vice, will guarantee a consistent measurement.

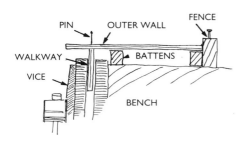

PIN OUTER WALL FENCE
WALKWAY BATTENS
VICE
BENCH

11 Glue and pin the parapet to the inner edge of the walkway, and trim the mitres at the corners with a saw or chisel.

Lay the walls together and tape them *(see page 44)*. Check that the walls will wrap around and meet, before applying glue to the mitre and pulling the walls together *(see page 44)*.

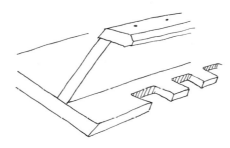

12 Locate the outer walls with pins or small glue blocks and glue them to the base. Fit the short lengths of walkway at the back of the castle and cut them square with the back wall to allow space for the keep.

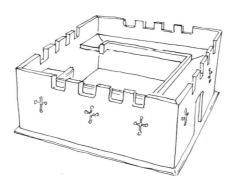

TOWERS

13 The towers are made from ³⁄₁₆in (4mm) MDF. The four sides of each tower are identical in size. To minimize time spent setting up the circular saw, and to eliminate dimensional variations, cut out all the sides for each tower at the same time.

Rout out the windows in all the sides.

Rout out the doors and the slots for the crenellations in half the sides.

Separate the pieces into groups to form towers, and mark on each side the position of each mitre. This does not matter with the outer walls, but the inner two walls of each tower have doors and slots, and here the doors should be at adjacent corners.

Rout the 45-degree mitres on all the sides.

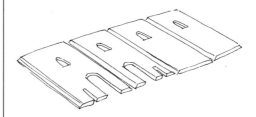

14 Tape and glue the towers together. Fit the towers in the corners. Measure and fit the square plate at the foot of each tower. This reinforces the corner joint and helps locate the tower. Glue the plates and the towers in position.

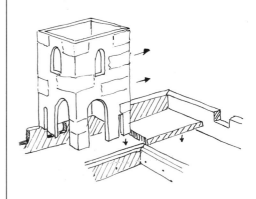

15 Cut four benches to conceal the tops of the battlements inside the tower, and glue them in place.

Cut eight floors to fit inside the towers: one each for the floor and one to glue to the underside of each roof. Support the floors on thin struts tucked into the corners of the tower. Rout out a hatchway to give access to the upper floor.

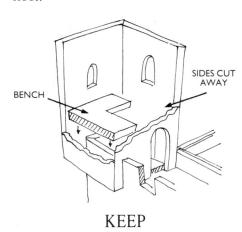

BENCH

SIDES CUT AWAY

KEEP

16 The keep is made from ¼in (6mm) MDF. Cut out the sides, rout out the crenellations, pillars, windows and doors and the 45-degree mitres for the two front corners.

Cut out the two floors and the hatchway in the top floor.

17 Tape and glue the sides of the keep and pin and glue the floors.

18 Fit the fireplace, walls and the doorway for the steps to the roof.

Fit the crenellations at the back of the keep. Fit the low wall at the back of the first floor.

Fit the door and hinges to close the back of the keep.

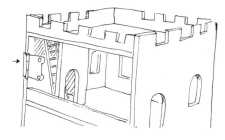

19 Make and fit the three towers. The large tower at the back of the keep has two floors. A ladder gives access to the first floor through a hatchway. There is no hatch into the upper room. If you have a tiny spinning wheel, this is where you should put it.

THE GATE, DRAWBRIDGE AND RAMP

20 The overhanging battlements of the gate are mitred, as is the front arched corner of the ramp. The twin pillars each side of the drawbridge are simple rectangles glued to the front wall of the castle.

21 The drawbridge is pivoted in the slot between the pillars and the blocks which are glued to the coping stones of the bridge. The pivot is a toothpick which protrudes ⅜in (9mm) on each side and is recessed into the back edge of the drawbridge.

The pivot lies between the blocks glued to the edge of the bridge and the front of the castle gate. The bridge should readily swing upwards to close the gate. If it does not, you may have to bevel the edges of the drawbridge next to the pivot.

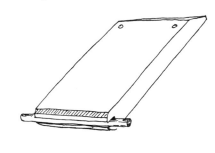

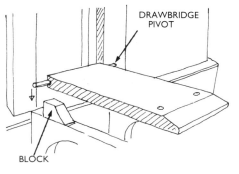

DRAWBRIDGE PIVOT

BLOCK

22 The winch is a ¼in (6mm) dowel which is held by two rectangular blocks glued to the inner walkway and the front castle wall. It is turned by stakes which fit through it. *(For advice on holding and drilling dowelling see page 14.)* The ramp is cut from a solid wood offcut and measures 5½in x 1¾in x 1⅜in (140mm x 45mm x 35mm).

ROOFS

23 Each tower has a pointed roof, truncated and rounded at the top for safety. These are easily cut to shape with a handsaw, planed smooth and then rounded at the top before being cut off at the eaves. The towers are of three sizes, all square in section: 2in x 2in (50mm x 50mm), 3in x 3in (75mm x 75mm) and 3½in x 3½in (90mm x 90mm). They can be made from any seasoned wood, and joined and made up from several pieces if necessary. Glue a surplus floor plate beneath each roof to locate the roof in position on the tower.

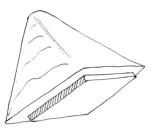

SPRAY PAINTING

The versatile electric spray gun illustrated is ideal for spray painting the castle and other toys. The container beneath the nozzle holds the paint supply, and the quantity of paint sprayed is adjusted by the knob at the back of the handle. A range of nozzles enables the spray gun to spray fluids of differing viscosities, from a thin, watery stain to a thick emulsion paint.

Before starting to spray, arrange excellent lighting and ventilation. For spraying most paints and stains you should wear a breathing mask. Use only spray paints and solvents with a flashpoint of 21°C (70°F) or above.

Mix the paints to the required thickness. If the paint is too thick the spray gun will not work. A simple viscosity gauge is supplied with the Bosch spray gun illustrated, which consists of a ladle with a small hole in its cup. Once you have selected the appropriate nozzle for the kind of paint you intend to spray, all you have to do is to measure the time it takes for a full ladle of paint to drain itself, and compare the results with the time chart provided with the gun. If necessary use an appropriate thinner.

Once the paint is the correct consistency, pour it into the paint container, and screw this back into the gun. Keep the gun level and hold it about 2ft (600mm) from a test piece. Press the trigger, and adjust the knob at the back of the handle until you achieve a fine, even and controllable spray. Move the gun horizontally, spraying across the test piece and past its edge. Do not change the direction of spray, or you will overload that part with too much paint.

When you are happy using the spray gun, spray the toy. Turn the toy round to present a fresh face after two applications of the spray. Plan each pass of the spray gun so that corners, ceilings, stairways and other awkward details are sprayed at the same rate as more accessible parts. Do not let the paint creep down the vertical surfaces.

Clean the spray gun immediately after use. Wash out the paint container and the ladle. Then pour a little thinner into the container, and spray the gun until the nozzle emits a clear spray. Remove the container, and wipe the suction tube clear of paint, and spray a little more fresh thinner through the gun. Wipe the gun, container and nozzles dry. Spray a little light oil through the gun if the paint has been thinned with water.

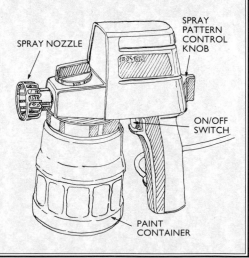

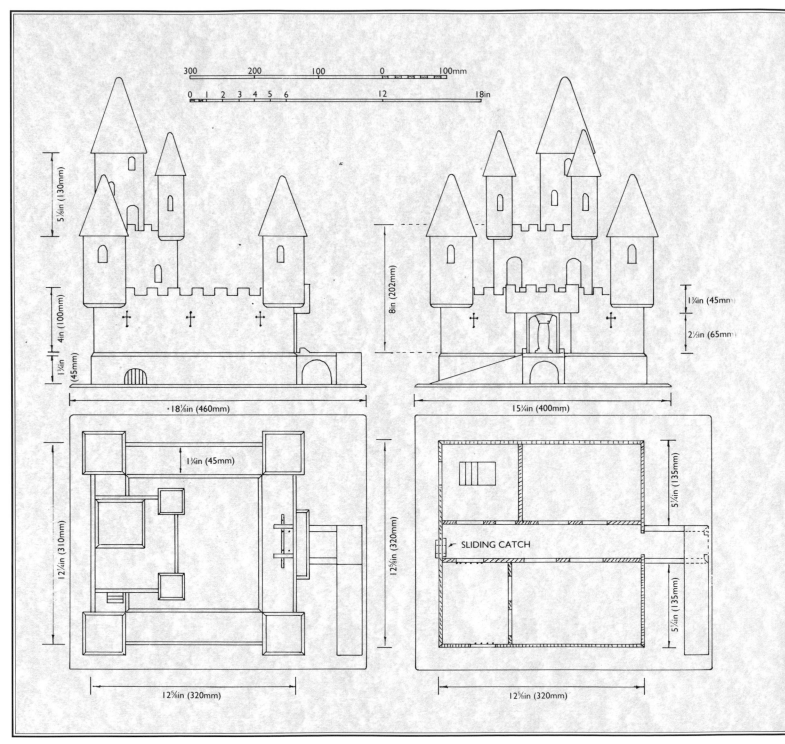

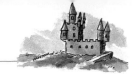

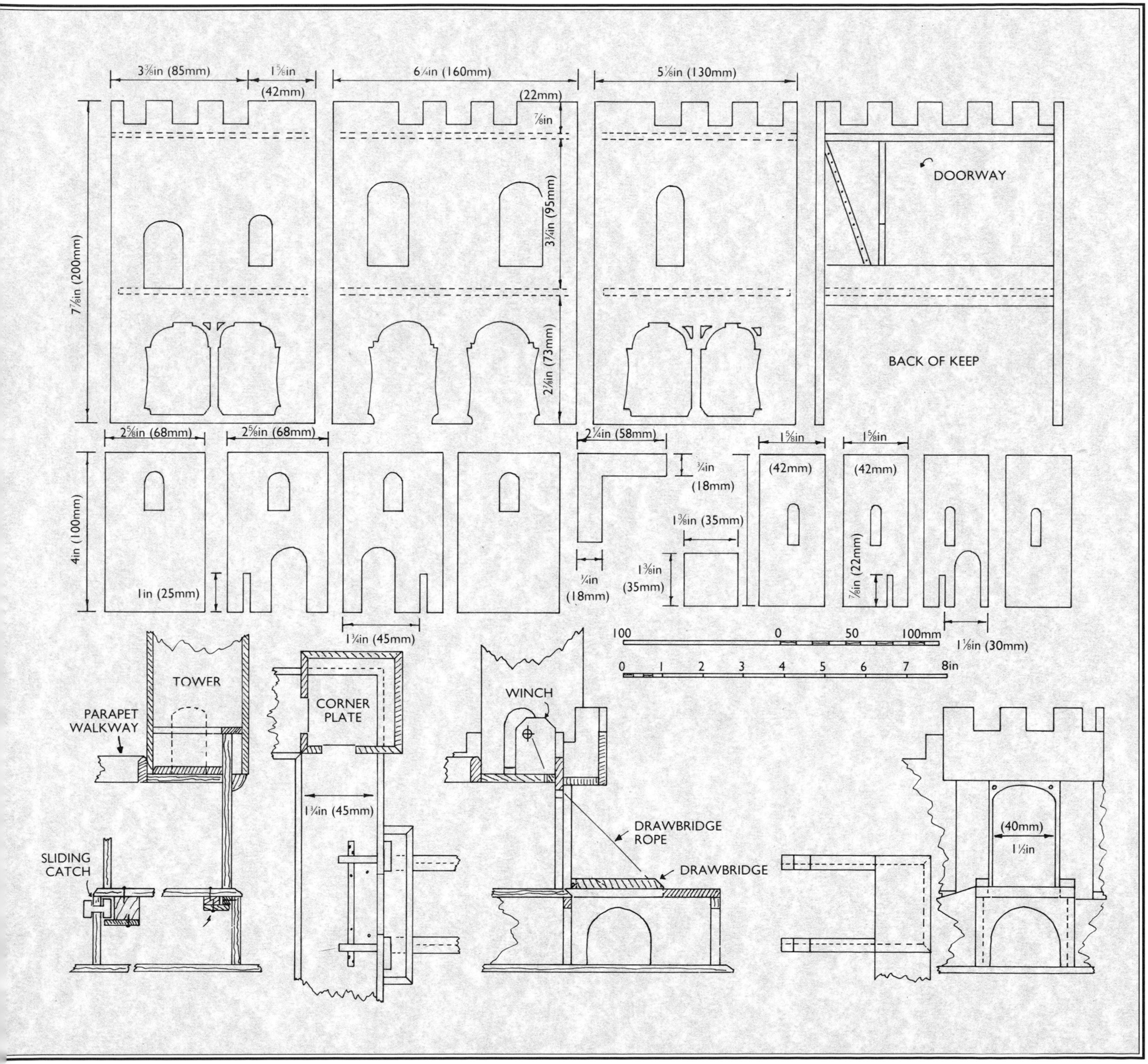
3⅜in (85mm)
1⅝in
(42mm)
6¼in (160mm)
(22mm)
⅞in
3¾in (95mm)
2⅞in (73mm)
5⅛in (130mm)
7⅞in (200mm)
DOORWAY
BACK OF KEEP
2⅝in (68mm)
2⅝in (68mm)
4in (100mm)
1in (25mm)
1¾in (45mm)
2¼in (58mm)
¾in
(18mm)
¾in
(18mm)
1⅜in (35mm)
1⅜in
(35mm)
1⅝in
(42mm)
1⅝in
(42mm)
⅞in (22mm)
1⅛in (30mm)
100
0
50
100mm
0
1
2
3
4
5
6
7
8in
TOWER
PARAPET
WALKWAY
SLIDING
CATCH
CORNER
PLATE
1¾in (45mm)
WINCH
DRAWBRIDGE
ROPE
DRAWBRIDGE
(40mm)
1½in

DOLL'S HOUSE

The terraced townhouse described and illustrated here is built to a scale of ¾ in =1ft (18mm =300mm). If you would prefer to construct a slightly larger doll's house, an alternative scale is indicated on the plans (1in= 1ft/25mm=300mm). Doll's house furniture does not need to be exactly in scale to look good, so commercially available furniture would be appropriate at either scale. Or you can make your own furniture, as described on pages 69-73. The advantage of the smaller scale is that the house does not become too big and heavy.

This house is easy to build. The stairs at the back are only suggested, and there are no vertical partitions between the rooms, no dividing doors, no banisters and no newel posts. And yet there is enough detail in this copy of a 19th-century toy to give any child or toymaker lasting pleasure. I could not resist the temptation of including a winch-driven dumb waiter and a back-lit staircase.

MATERIALS

¼in (6mm) birch-faced plywood
³⁄₁₆in (4mm) MDF offcuts
2in x ¾in (50mm x 18mm) pine strip
1in x 1in (25mm x 25mm) pine
⅝in (15mm) dowel
¹⁄₁₆in (2mm) balsa or pine strip
8 x ½in (12mm) doll's house hinges
2 x 1½in (40mm) cranked hinges
(⅛in) 3.2mm clear acrylic sheet
Postcard

TOOLS

Jigsaw, lathe, pillar drill, lathe for turning columns and knobs, electric glue gun, long-nosed pliers, small, fine-toothed hacksaw

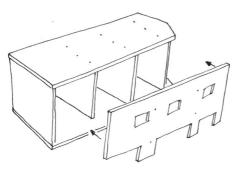

1 Mark out all of the large plywood components on the plywood sheet before beginning to cut them out. Allow ³⁄₁₆in (4mm) for the thickness of the saw-cut. Tack together those components which share identical dimensions and trim them as one unit with a plane, taking great care to maintain strict dimensional control over each component.

2 When all the main pieces are cut to size, mark on the inner wall A the doors and the hatches for the dumb waiter. Note that because the doors are situated so close to the side wall, the doorpost holding the door hinges is glued directly to the side wall. This greatly simplifies the task of cutting out the doorways.

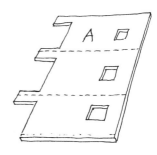

3 Cut out the hatches and doorways with a jigsaw or fretsaw, and file them square. Mark on the back wall the location of each floor and ceiling and

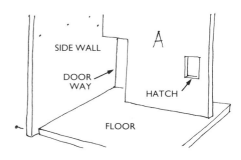

extend the line across on the inner wall with a set square.

4 Place the sides and back together and transfer the marks to the inside of the side walls. Note that the bottom floor fits inside the side walls and the inner wall A.

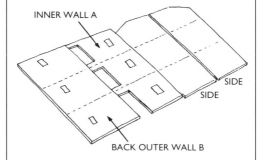

INNER WALL A

SIDE

SIDE

BACK OUTER WALL B

5 When the marking is complete, square round on the outside of the side walls the centre line of each floor and drive two veneer pins into each line as illustrated. The pins should emerge through the plywood and grip the floors as they are glued and nailed in position.

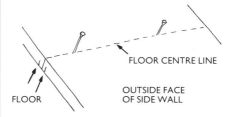

FLOOR CENTRE LINE

OUTSIDE FACE OF SIDE WALL

FLOOR

6 Glue and nail the main structure together with PVA glue. When both sides are glued and held by the pins at each floor, fit the inner wall. This should give stability to the construction, and bring it square. Check that everything has fitted together properly before driving in any more veneer pins to lock the building together.

7 Fit one side of the dumb-waiter shaft. Insert temporary spacer blocks inside the shaft while you glue the second side, to ensure that the shaft sides remain straight and parallel. Cut and fit the short lengths of floor that reach to the side of the shaft. Note that the sides of the shaft and the floor are the same width, which is 1³⁄₈in (35mm), ¹⁄₄in (6mm) narrower than the space between the back of the inner wall and the edge of the sides. This difference allows the back outer wall B to fit inside the sides.

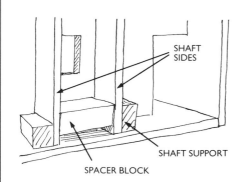

SHAFT SIDES

SHAFT SUPPORT

SPACER BLOCK

8 Now cut the blocks which make up the first steps of each flight of stairs and glue them in position. The steps can only be seen from the front of the house, and once they have turned the corner and are out of sight, you can stop adding them.

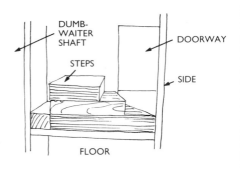

9 Cut out the dumb waiter and assemble it.

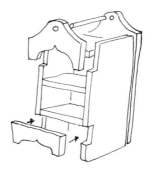

10 Make the winch, which sits on the attic floor, positioned in line with the hole in the right-hand end gable.

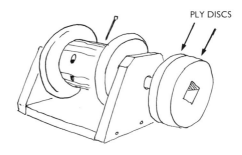

11 Once the dumb waiter is connected to its hoist, and you are confident that the winch system works, fit the triangular plywood slabs to the inside of the end gables and glue the two roof plates in position, with the hatch directly above the winch.

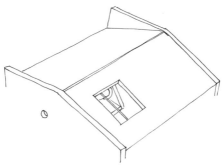

12 Glue the chimney stack to the back of the roof. Bevel the underside of the cornice moulding, and drill in it the three ⅜in (9mm) holes for the chimney pots.

13 Taper the chimney pots with a chisel and sandpaper, and then glue them into the cornice moulding and glue the moulding to the top of the chimney stack.

14 Fit the back wall B and hold it in position with masking tape. The remaining work inside the house, although detailed and in some places rather inaccessible, is not difficult. Techniques for carrying out the main detailing work, including fitting doors, skirtings, architrave, mouldings and fireplaces, are described and illustrated below.

ARCHITECTURAL FEATURES

15 Use soft, easily cut, straight-grained wood for the linings, skirtings and other features of the house. Balsa wood is ideal because it can be cut with a scalpel, glues readily with cellulose-based modelling cement and can be obtained planed from most model-making shops.

DOORS

16 Make the doors from ¼in (6mm) plywood. Each door fits inside its doorway and is hinged to a ¼in (6mm) square doorpost, which is then glued to the side wall.

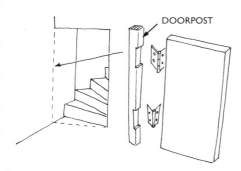

17 Fit the doorpost. The door should be a little shorter than the doorpost so that it opens and shuts easily. Position the hinges on the edge of the door as illustrated and nail them in position. Although the hinge

manufacturers provide the hinges with oversize holes to allow for adjustment, it is a good idea to mark the centre of each hole with a pencil and then punch it with a veneer pin held in the jaws of long-nosed pliers before driving in the nails which will secure the hinge.

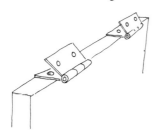

18 Once the hinges are fixed to the door, mark their exact location on the doorpost and cut out a recess on the inside of the doorpost for each hinge. The recess should be slightly shallower than the overall thickness of the hinge when it is closed.

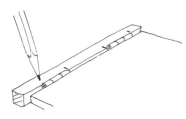

19 Cut the recess in two operations: first cut across the grain with a small metalworking hacksaw, then chop out the waste with a very sharp chisel

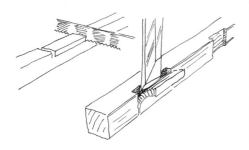

held vertically. Now position the hinges in the slots and check that everything is satisfactory by inserting both the door and the doorpost.

20 Typical problems and their remedies are illustrated below. When a good fit is achieved, spot some cellulose-based modelling cement in the recesses and wedge the door and, doorpost in position. Once the glue has dried, remove the assembly and, following the same procedure as before, hammer in the four nails, securing the two hinges to the doorpost.

Now cut out and glue the cardboard strips to the front and back of the door, and drill and fit the two doorknobs. *(For instructions on turning the knobs see page 64.)*

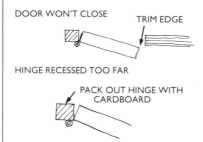

DOOR WON'T CLOSE   TRIM EDGE

HINGE RECESSED TOO FAR

PACK OUT HINGE WITH CARDBOARD

21 Glue the doorpost in position with PVA glue. Hold the door by inserting a couple of wedges to press the doorpost in position.

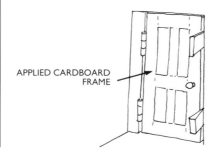

APPLIED CARDBOARD FRAME

ARCHITRAVES

22 Fit the architraves once the doors are in position and before the skirting boards are fitted. Strips measuring ¼in x ¹⁄₁₆in (6mm x 2mm) are needed, mitred at the corners. Slots must be chopped out from the edge of the architrave on the doorposts so that the hinges fit. The inside edges of the architrave should be flush with, or slightly set back from, the edge of the doorway. The architrave should never overlap this edge, since this could obstruct the door.

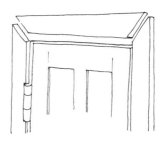

SKIRTINGS

23 Make the skirtings from ½in x ¹⁄₁₆in (12mm x 2mm) strip. A simple moulding can be made near the top edge of each strip with the home-made tool illustrated below. The joints are all straightforward, sawn with a tenon saw or fine-toothed hacksaw and trimmed with a chisel. Samples of the joints are illustrated.

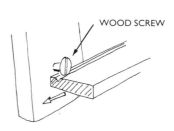

WOOD SCREW

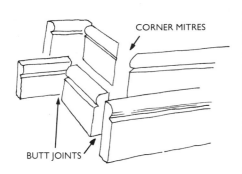

CORNER MITRES

BUTT JOINTS

MOULDINGS

24 Slightly more complicated mouldings than that described above can be fashioned by altering the setting of the screw on the improvised gauge. Where more ornamental mouldings are required, for example in the mantelpiece supports illustrated on the right, they can be cut from a solid piece of pine with a fretsaw. Alternatively, you might find a suitable section of commercial moulding strip in your local hardware shop. Examples of some useful mouldings are illustrated on the right below.

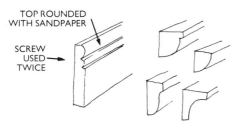

TOP ROUNDED WITH SANDPAPER

SCREW USED TWICE

FIREPLACES

25 Ornamental fireplaces are available from shops which specialize in doll's houses and their furnishings *(see page 142)*. The fireplaces featured in this house are very easy to make, and their simple

components are illustrated below. Note that the mason's mitres on the lintel of the kitchen and drawing-room fireplaces are stopped and a nick is made at the ends of the moulding to indicate false mitres.

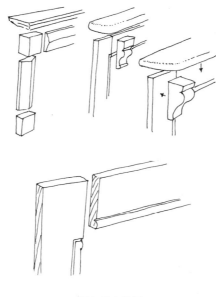

FAÇADE

26 The work required to create the gracious façade is intricate and should be completed before the front of the doll's house is fitted.

Using a sharp hard pencil, draw on the façade the position of each strip of applied stonework and the centre line for each window bar. Make a list of the sizes of the strips you will need. Assemble a stock of strips, preferably of balsa wood, so that once you have started you will not be interrupted by the need for fresh supplies. Use a contact adhesive or a cellulose-based modelling cement for glueing on these thin pieces of wood.

Apply the outer strips (½in x ³⁄₁₆in/12mm x 4mm), laying the bottom strip first, running it under the doorway and stopping it short at the sides by a distance equal to the width of the garden walls (⅜in/9mm). Next fit the two vertical strips, and then the top horizontal strip, with its two ⅜in (9mm) filler pieces at the outer edges of the wall. Add the doubling piece to the top front strip, and then the decorative ¼in (6mm) square on top of that.

The next job is to complete the work on the windows.

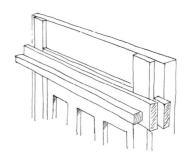

WINDOWS

27 Glue the ¹⁄₁₆in (2mm) strip inside each window frame, keeping the front edge of the strips flush with the outer face of the house. This strip will

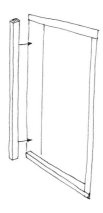

retain the window glass and give a clean sharp outline to the window.

28 Fit the horizontal strips first, and hold them in position with tight-fitting vertical strips.

Cut out the glazing bars for each window, trimming them to length with a chisel to make certain that they provide a tight press fit. Use the marks on the perimeter of each window to position the bars, and make a pencil mark on the vertical bar where the horizontal bar crosses it.

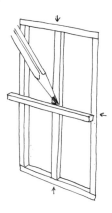

29 A simple cross-halving joint connects the two bars. Make two cuts in the vertical bar just inside the marks you have made. The cuts should not go deeper than halfway through the glazing bar. You will find that a sharp scalpel is an ideal tool if your glazing bars are made from balsa wood. Remove the waste from between the two cuts with the tip of the scalpel or a fine chisel and repeat the procedure on the horizontal bar. The resulting joint should appear as illustrated below. Align the vertical glazing bar with the marks on the edge of the window frame and glue it in position. Spot the ends and the slot in

the centre of the horizontal bar with PVA glue and fit it in place. Fit the glazing bars on the remaining windows in the same way. Ensure that the bars are fitted perpendicularly to each other and that they line up with the bars in all of the other windows.

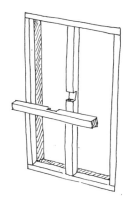

30 Now fit the window ledges, the two vertical strips each side of each window and the decorative lintels.

The glazing bars of the semicircular window over the front door are not individually cut and jointed. The entire window frame and the bars are cut out with a fretsaw from a small scrap of ³⁄₁₆in (4mm) MDF. *(For instructions on using a fretsaw see pages 127-8.)*

The outer shape of the window is traced by holding the scrap against the window aperture and pencilling around the perimeter of the frame. Mark the front face of the scrap piece and mark in the glazing bars. Glue the paper template to the MDF, ready for sawing.

Cut the curved perimeter glazing bars and then the inner segments. The waste MDF beneath the horizontal glazing bars provides a useful handhold when you are shaping and carving the window, so do not cut it off until the

frame fits in the space above the doorway. Bevel the outer facing edges of the bars and file away any major irregularities, then cut off the waste below the horizontal glazing bar at the bottom of the window.

31 Using a sharp knife or chisel, strip away ¹⁄₁₆in (2mm) of the thickness of the bars, to bring the overall thickness of the strips to ¹⁄₁₆in (2mm). Make a template of the outer shape of the window so that later you will be able to cut out the acrylic sheet for the window. Glue the window bars in position, set back from the front face of the building by ¹⁄₁₆in (2mm). Now fit the top of the door frame beneath the window, pressing it into position with the two doorposts, which rest on the doorstep. Note that the doorposts, window, glazing bars and top of the door frame are all set back from the front face of the building by ¹⁄₁₆in (2mm).

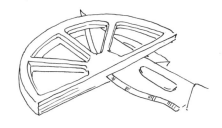

32 The decorative stonework pillar is applied slightly set back from the sawn edge of the doorway, giving a stepped effect when seen in plan.

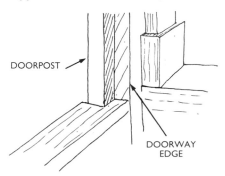

DOORPOST

DOORWAY EDGE

GLAZING

33 The window panes are cut from a sheet of ⅛in (3.2mm) clear acrylic. The upper panes are 2in x 3¾in (58mm x 95mm) and the kitchen windows are 2¼in x 3in (58mm x 75mm), and you must use the template of the glazing bars for the window pane over the front door. Fit the windows, planing the acrylic to size if necessary. Glue the windows in position after the house has been painted and decorated.

FRONT DETAILS

34 Nail and glue the front garden to the underside of the façade. Mark in the position for the front steps, the column plinths and the low stone wall which borders the steps. Cut out the components for the steps, the coping stones, the side walls and the plinths. If you make them in pairs, you will save time and trouble.

Cut out the recesses in the plinths and mark and drill the centres with a ³⁄₁₆in

(4mm) bit. Now glue one low wall, plinth and coping stone. Next fit the steps and then press into position the opposite wall, coping and plinth. When the steps are in place, the applied decoration around the doorway can be completed.

Turn the two columns. *(Instructions on turning are given on pages 133-8.)* If you do not have a lathe, fashion the columns from ¾in (18mm) dowel. Taper them with a small block plane at the top and sand them smooth with 90-grit sandpaper backed by a polyethylene-foam pad. The rings at the top and bottom of the column can be reproduced by winding thread around the columns and then brushing the thread with PVA glue. Bore a ³⁄₁₆in (4mm) centre hole in the ends of each column and cut and fit a short length of dowel or nail into the holes. These protrusions will locate the ends of the column in the plinth and in the porch above.

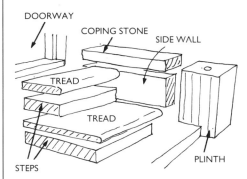

DOORWAY

COPING STONE

SIDE WALL

TREAD

TREAD

STEPS

PLINTH

35 Now cut out the porch roof, nail and glue on the sides and glue the decorative strip around the front and sides. Mark in the position for the centre of each column. Sight this very carefully before drilling the two holes. The columns need to be vertical as seen from

the side as well as from the front of the house. Since they are a distinctive feature, errors in their alignment will be instantly noticeable.

Once the holes for the tops of the columns have been drilled, the complete porch can be assembled. Lay the façade flat on the workbench and glue the porch and columns in position. Hold them in position with weights.

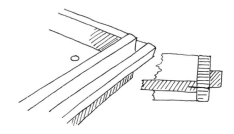

RAILINGS, WALL AND FENCE

36 The railings and the low garden wall are both ¼in (6mm) wide, so the easiest way to make the fence is to cut a strip of pine for the wall measuring 1½in x ¼in x 24in (40mm x 6mm x 600mm), which includes enough additional wood in its section for the railings. Mark along the top of the strip the ⅜in (9mm) centres for the railings. Arrange a fence on the pillar-drill table to position the drill automatically down the centre of the strip, and drill the holes for the fence. Cut off the railings strip from the low wall, plane off the saw marks and bevel the edges of the wall. Cut enough toothpicks, matchsticks or bamboo barbecue sticks to make the palings, and assemble the fence. Before dabbing a few spots of PVA glue on the top of the wall and under the railings to fix them in position, check that the

railings and the wall are parallel. If they are not, you will have difficulty joining sections together.

Once the glue has dried, trim about ³⁄₁₆in (4mm) from the end of the wall and fit the end of the railings against the side of the pillar. Cut off the wall and railings where they meet the edge of the garden.

37 Repeat the procedure on the opposite side of the front

doorway, and then mark and chisel a 45-degree mitre on both the wall and the railings. Fit the returns in the same way, this time cutting the mitres first before cutting the butt joint to fit against the façade of the house. Glue the front garden fence in place. Hold the butt joints with masking tape and the mitres at the corners with a twist of fine wire, which can be removed after the glue has completely dried.

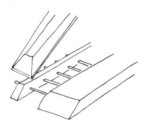

TILING

38 The tiles are made from thin cardboard, and laying them is much easier if they are all the same length and width. You will need some half-width tiles with which to start and finish alternate courses. Ensure good ventilation if you glue the tiles with cellulose-based modelling cement. The ridge tiles are also of cardboard and each covers two roofing tiles.

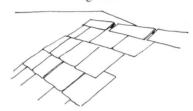

TURNING DOORKNOBS

Doorknobs can be turned from short lengths of ¼in (6mm) dowel, using an electric drill. Hold the drill in the woodworking vice.

Clamp it tightly, but not so hard as to damage the plastic or aluminium casting. Position the chuck so that when the dowel is fitted into the chuck it is just about level with the

edge of the vice.

Take a sharp ⅛in (4mm) chisel, and switch on the electric drill. First, trim a radius on the end of the dowel,

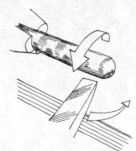

and then, using the corner of the chisel, complete the shaping at the back of the knob.

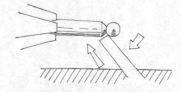

With a penknife, incise a shoulder line just behind the knob.

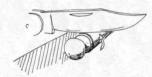

Then with the chisel reduce the waste behind the shoulder line to ⅛in (4mm) diameter.

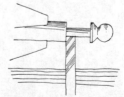

Sandpaper the knob, remove it from the drill chuck, and separate it from the rest of the dowel with a saw or penknife. Drill a ⅛in (4mm) hole in the door, and glue the knob on.

GLUES AND SCREWS

GLUES

PVA glue

This is a white liquid which hardens to a clear solid, forming a strong, slightly elastic waterproof bond. Excess glue can be wiped away with a stiff brush dipped in water.

A disadvantage of most PVA glues is that when the glue is spread on two wooden surfaces which are then pressed together, the glue acts as a lubricant, so that it is difficult to align the pieces of wood accurately. Most of the toys described in this book are constructed with a combination of PVA glue and nails or screws. This technique is effective because the points of the nails or screws secure the wood while the pieces are slid into place.

Epoxy resin

This is a tough, weatherproof glue. With the addition of different fillers, it can serve as a gap filler, viscous glue, or high-build clear varnish. The 'Speedipack' system, marketed by S P Systems Ltd (see page 142) is recommended for use in these projects. It is ideal for toy makers because the resin and hardener are dispensed in accurate proportions from pumps on the containers.

The addition of colloidal silica enhances the gap-filling qualities of epoxy resin without diminishing the strength of the glue join. Gaps of up to ¼in (6mm) can be bridged with epoxy resin without loss of strength. Colloidal silica is also obtainable from S P Systems.

Cellulose-based modelling cement

This is a clear, quick-drying liquid glue which is ideal for fixing thin wooden, cardboard or paper decorations to the toys. It is dispensed from a tube. Use the glue in a well-ventilated area.

Contact adhesive

This is a solvent-based glue which is ideal for glueing wood quickly where great strength is not essential. Choose a thixotropic, non-stringy variety. Apply a thin layer of glue to both surfaces to be joined, and press them together when the glue is touch dry. Most contact adhesives allow some small readjustments of position before the glue sets.

Electric glue gun

In certain situations an electric glue gun is invaluable. It can be used to instantly glue or weld applied decorations, to hold awkward pieces of wood for shaping and to keep pieces temporarily in position. It is also useful for accurate glueing, provided you preheat the surfaces to be joined. If they are not preheated there will be insufficient time between applying the glue and clamping the joint, to achieve a close or accurate bond.

SCREWS

Slotted countersunk and round-headed screws are the two types of screw used in making these toys. They are available in steel, brass or black-japanned steel. You must always pre-drill the work before you screw it together, drilling a shank hole the full length of the screw, and a pilot hole for the shank. A countersunk head requires one further drilling operation to make the conical recess for the screw head. This is done with a countersink bit.

Always try to match the top of the screw with the size of the screwdriver. The two should be of similar width, otherwise either the screwdriver will chew up the top of the screw, or it will overhang it and damage the adjacent wood.

Provided that the pilot holes are properly drilled, the problems encountered with screwing are almost entirely due to faults with the screwdriver. Its tip should be ground flat and straight. If it is sharpened or rounded, the screwdriver will jump out of the slot onto the timber, or it will cut into the slot of the screw and create sharp metal splinters.

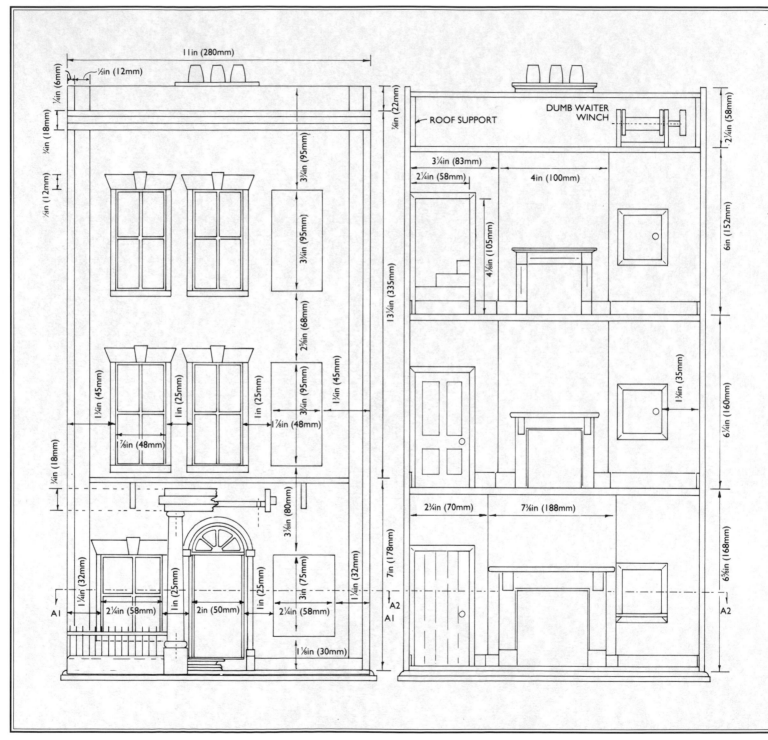

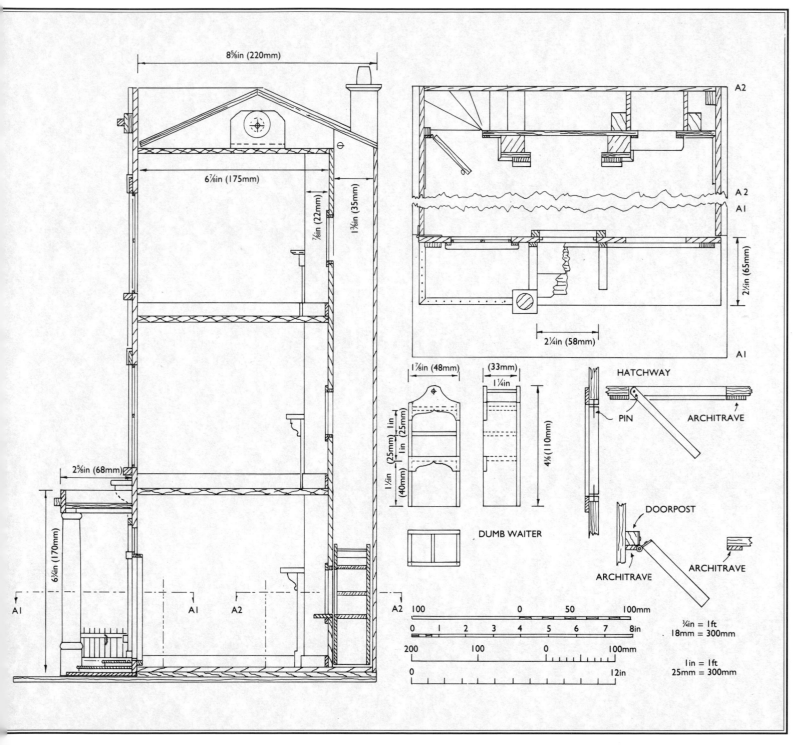

8⅝in (220mm)

6⅞in (175mm)

⅞in (22mm)

1⅜in (35mm)

2⅝in (68mm)

6¾in (170mm)

A1

A1

A2

A2

A2

A2

A1

A1

2½in (65mm)

2¼in (58mm)

1⅞in (48mm)

(33mm)

1¼in

1in
(25mm)

1in
(25mm)

1in

1½in
(40mm)

4⅜in (110mm)

DUMB WAITER

HATCHWAY

PIN

ARCHITRAVE

DOORPOST

ARCHITRAVE

ARCHITRAVE

100   0   50   100mm

0   1   2   3   4   5   6   7   8in

200   100   0   100mm

0   12in

¾in = 1ft
18mm = 300mm

1in = 1ft
25mm = 300mm

DOLL'S HOUSE
FURNITURE

Doll's house furniture does not need to be exactly in scale with the house to look right. Some of the appeal of a furnished doll's house lies in the inventive attempts to reproduce real items at such a small scale. For example, a postage stamp in a frame of mitred matchsticks makes a good picture. No special tools are called for, although a lathe would be useful if you would prefer to turn the central pillar of the pedestal table.

PEDESTAL TABLE

MATERIALS

2in x 2in x ¼in (50mm x 50mm x 6mm) hardwood
½in (12mm) dowel or hardwood spindle

Cut the top from a piece of smooth hardwood. Cut the support strip to size, bore a ¼in (6mm) hole in its centre and glue it across the grain on the underside of the table.

Turn or carve the pedestal, trim one end to fit into the hole in the support strip and chisel three flat surfaces at the bottom end for the legs.

Cut and smooth the legs and glue them in place with instant glue.

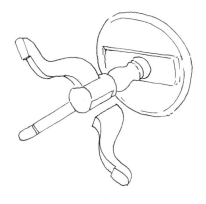

KITCHEN DRESSER

MATERIALS

³⁄₁₆in (4mm) MDF
⁵⁄₈in x 1⅛in (15mm x 30mm) pine
¼in (6mm) dowel

The plate rack of this dresser is held to the top of the dresser base by two veneer pins, set in the top of the dresser, with their points pressed into the ends of the plate rack. The four front legs of the base are made from lengths of ¼in (6mm) dowel, slightly tapered. Notice that the holes and recesses in the pot board are duplicated exactly in the board glued to the underside of the dresser. The drawers are false, defined at the top and bottom by the two ³⁄₁₆in (4mm) MDF boards and at the sides by shallow sawcuts made with a fine tenon saw or hacksaw.

DRESSER BASE
Cut the three MDF boards to size. Chamfer the sides and front of the top board to form the moulded edge of the top, and sand a slight radius on the front

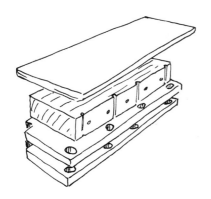

edge and sides of the two lower boards. Align these two boards, pin them together and mark and drill the slots for the back legs and then the four ¼in (6mm) holes for the front legs.

Cut out the ½in (12mm) thick centrepiece which is sandwiched between the two top boards, and saw the imitation drawer sides in it. Use contact adhesive to glue the three pieces of the dresser base together.

Cut and chamfer the four front legs, and fit them through the pot board and into the underside of the dresser base. Fit and glue the two rectangular-section back legs.

PLATE RACK
The rack is glued together with contact adhesive. Mark the positions for the shelves on the two sides. Cut the shelves and cornice piece to size, chamfer the cornice and glue the rack together.

With the rack held in position over the base, mark in the locations for the two pins which hold it in place. Make the holes for the two rack fastening pins by hammering a veneer pin into each mark. Withdraw the pins with pliers. Cut the heads from two pins and, holding them with long-nosed pliers, drive the blunt end of each pin into the top of the base in the positions previously marked. Leave about ¼in (6mm) of each pin poking out of the top of the dresser. Lay the dresser and the rack on a flat surface and press the rack against the sharp pins until the rack is tight against the top of the dresser base.

With the dresser still on its back, hammer in the gimp pins to form the drawer knobs.

BOOKCASE

MATERIALS

¹⁄₁₆in (2mm) plywood

Cut out the components. All of the pieces are the same thickness and the sides, bottom and shelves are the same width, but not the top and back.

Mark on the sides the position of the undersides of the shelves and the bottom. Glue a short length of matchstick against the lines marking the bottom on the back, and on the two sides, and when the glue is dry, glue the bottom shelf into position on top of the matchsticks. Now fit the remaining shelves, applying glue to the sides and back of each one as they are fitted. Glue the top on.

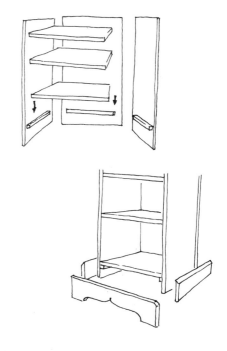

Use a fretsaw to cut out the frieze at the base of the bookcase. Glue a couple of plain wooden returns at the base of the sides, concealing their ends by glueing the frieze at the front.

SETTLE

> ## MATERIALS
>
> ¼in x 1in (6mm x 25mm) pine strips

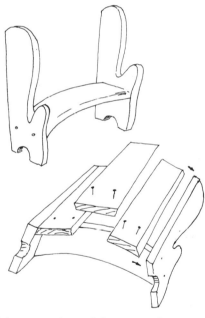

Make a template of the seat and one side. Cut out two sides and one seat and round their front edges. Pin and glue the sides to the seat. Take the strips for the back and plane the side of the first strip so that it slips neatly against the side of the settle, and glue it in place. Do the same with a strip on the other side. Plane the middle strip so that it slips between the two outer strips and closes the back.

COOKING RANGE

> ## MATERIALS
>
> ³⁄₁₆in (4mm) MDF
> ¼in (6mm) MDF
> ⅜in (9mm) dowel

The oven door of this traditional cooking range is hinged by a simple pivot system using two pins. One is driven into the underside of the door and the other down through the top of the cooker into the top of the door. Note that although the front sides and top of the cooker are made from ³⁄₁₆in (4mm) MDF, the oven door and base are made from ¼in (6mm) MDF.

Cut the component pieces to size. Cut or rout the inside mitres on the four sides (*see pages 131-3*) and, using a fretsaw, cut out the hole in the front for the oven. Round off the edges of the base with sandpaper and chamfer and round off the edges of the top.

Clamp the top and base together and drill the pivot hole for the oven door through them both.

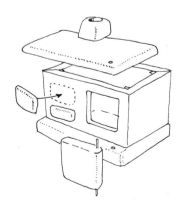

Glue the sides, taping the pieces together in a strip and then applying the glue, before bringing the two ends together and taping them (*see page 44*).

Glue the sides to the base and glue the top in position. Cut out and fit the two false fronts for the ashpan and firebox and cut out the oven door. Hold the door in place and mark in the position of the pivot holes. Drill these with a veneer pin before driving one pin into the bottom of the door and pressing it into position in the cooker base. Check that the door opens and closes freely before driving a second pin through the top of the cooker into the door.

Drill, shape and glue the flue box.

REFECTORY TABLE

> ## MATERIALS
>
> 2in x ³⁄₁₆in (50mm x 4mm) plywood

Cut out the components, glue them and slot them together. If you prefer, you can make the table look like old wood by staining and then varnishing it.

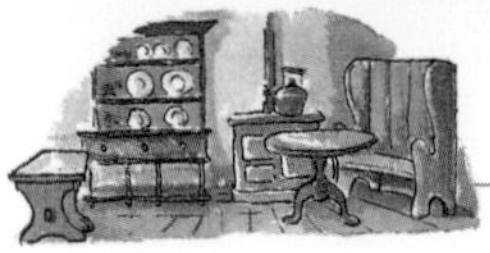

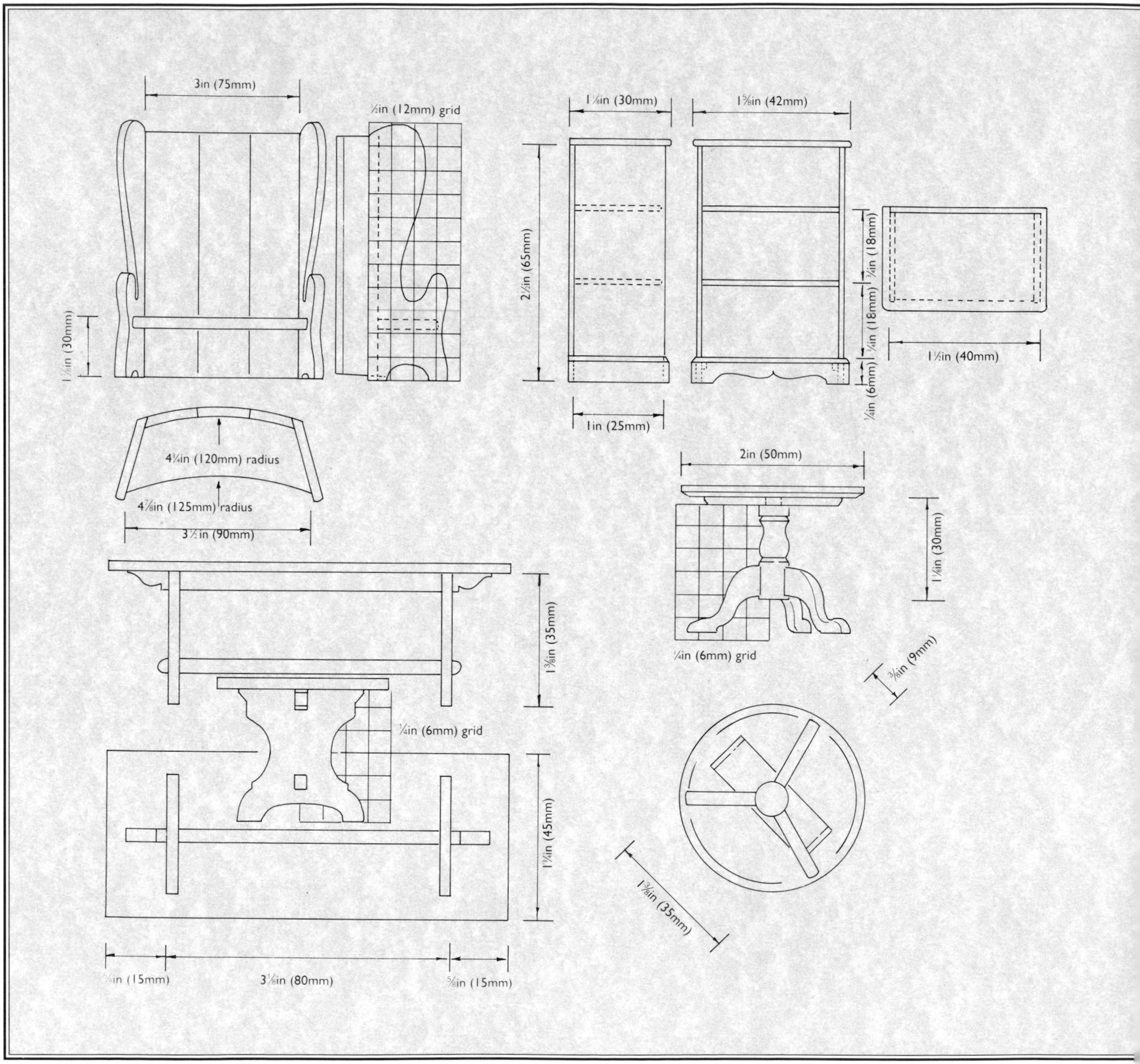
3in (75mm)
½in (12mm) grid
1¼in (30mm)
4¾in (120mm) radius
4⅞in (125mm) radius
3½in (90mm)
1¼in (30mm)
1⅝in (42mm)
2½in (65mm)
¾in (18mm)
¾in (18mm)
¼in (6mm)
1in (25mm)
1½in (40mm)
2in (50mm)
1¼in (30mm)
¼in (6mm) grid
⅜in (9mm)
1⅜in (35mm)
1⅜in (35mm)
¼in (6mm) grid
1¾in (45mm)
⅝in (15mm)
3⅛in (80mm)
⅝in (15mm)

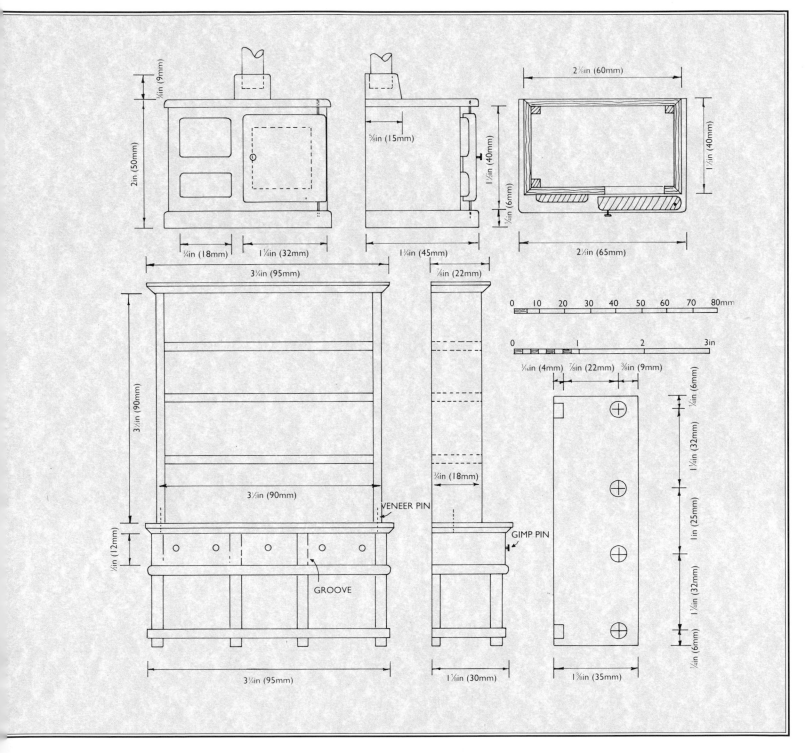

⅜in (9mm)

2in (50mm)

⅝in (15mm)

2⅜in (60mm)

1⅝in (40mm)

1⅝in (40mm)

¼in (6mm)

¾in (18mm)

1¼in (32mm)

1¾in (45mm)

⅞in (22mm)

2½in (65mm)

3¾in (95mm)

3½in (90mm)

3½in (90mm)

0 10 20 30 40 50 60 70 80mm

0   1   2   3in

⅛in (4mm)   ⅞in (22mm)   ⅜in (9mm)

¼in (6mm)

¾in (18mm)

1¼in (32mm)

1in (25mm)

1¼in (32mm)

¼in (6mm)

½in (12mm)

VENEER PIN

GROOVE

GIMP PIN

3¾in (95mm)

1⅛in (30mm)

1⅜in (35mm)

BOATS

TUGBOAT

Like the battleship and the paddle steamer, the tugboat is designed to float. The hollow hull of each boat consists of a sandwich of hollowed slabs, stacked and glued together and then carved on the outside.

The tugboat has a flush deck, a simple deckhouse with a hatch and railings at the stern. The funnel is mounted on the deckhouse and slots over a short stub of dowel so that it can be removed. This tugboat has a full rounded hull and floats quite high in the water. You can vary the deck layout and add details such as winches, cabins, guns or cranes.

MATERIALS

4¾in x 1in (120mm x 25mm) pine plank
³⁄₁₆in (4mm) marine plywood offcuts
¾in x ¾in (18mm x 18mm) pine offcuts
³⁄₁₆in (4mm) dowel
¼in (6mm) dowel
Epoxy resin glue

TOOLS

Jigsaw, pillar drill with ½in (12mm) brad-point bit, belt sander with bench-mounting bracket, carving gouges: No 4 (16mm), No 8 (8mm), No 10 (4mm)

1 Use the grid on the plan drawing to make a half-plan template of the hull. Draw a centre line down the 4¾in (120mm) plank and, using the template of the hull plan, draw three complete hull shapes along the centre line.

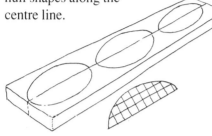

2 The hull is built as a sandwich. The bottom slab is left solid, but the centres of the two upper pieces should be removed with a jigsaw. The illustrations show the different cutting patterns for the two upper layers. The noticeable differences are due to the variations in hull shape at the different levels in the hull.

Cut around the outline of each layer. Drill a ½in (12mm) hole in the waste part of the two upper slabs, feed the jigsaw blade through each hole and cut out the centre cores.

Now glue the three layers together, using plenty of glue. Stack them together and hold them in place with a weight. The glue fills gaps and there is no advantage to be gained by squeezing it from between the layers.

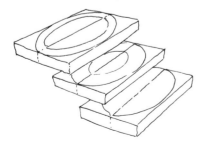

3 Trim the hull to shape. Check that the pencilled centre lines at the ends of the top layer and along the bottom are intact. Use the template to re-establish the deck line on the top layer. Now use a bench-mounted belt sander, or a plane and a rasp, to smooth the sides of the hull. Remove all the saw marks and misalignments on the outside.

You will need some lines to guide you when you carve the hull shape. This may seem a rather daunting task, but if you do it carefully and slowly you will find it a pleasure.

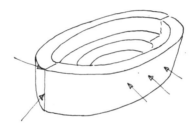

4 The three most useful pieces of advice I can offer on carving are:
- Use sharp tools *(see advice on sharpening on pages 130-1)*.
- Each cut removes its own shaving.
- Know the shape you aim to create. This last point needs further explanation. We all think we know what a boat looks like, but faced with a lozenge-shaped block and a gouge, we might begin to have doubts, especially when the first gouge cuts seem to have ruined what was a perfectly serviceable if unattractive hull. It helps to bear in mind the following points:
- There are parts of the hull which need no further carving. Those parts are finished and can be defined by pencil as in the illustration above.
- Any alterations in shape must be gradual and smooth, so work away from the finished parts, removing progressively less wood as you work towards another finished area.
- Boats are symmetrical, so that both sides underwater are the same. Therefore work on one side to explore the technique, then duplicate your work on the other side before you forget what you have done.
- Learn to sight your work as it progresses. Stand back and view the piece from all angles – and be critical. If you do not like what you have done, simply alter it.
- Never undercut. You can only correct a carving mistake if you have not already removed wood from behind what you are shaping. Provided enough wood remains to allow you to carve deeper, you can rescue your work. *(There is more advice on carving on page 82. Suggestions for using and sharpening gouges and chisels are given on pages 129-31 and an appropriate gap-filling paste, if required, is described on page 65.)*

STAGES IN CARVING

5 Inspect the inside of the hull carefully. Note where there is ample wood to carve and where (as at the top sides) there is little. When the boat is upside down, you will have to remember how much wood you have to work with.

Make up a carving board as illustrated. The coach bolt pivots the board to the bench, and the washer and wingnut clamp it in position. The boat is held to the board with two countersunk screws driven in from beneath the board.

Screw the boat to the board (capturing the bolt before doing so) and then poke the bolt through a hole in the bench, and tighten the wingnut.

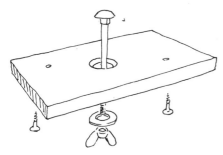

6 Use the No 8 gouge to carve the bow as illustrated. First remove the hard corners at the edge of the hull, cutting in a diagonal direction as illustrated below. Avoid cutting away the stem and keel – these should be left until the shaping on both sides is almost complete. Increase the width of the bevel as you approach the point of the bow. When the sides are symmetrical when viewed from the front, remove the edges of the bevel with a second layer of cuts, as below, and then a third, until the hull curves from its flat bottom into the vertical side, as in the third illustration.

SIDE VIEW

FRONT VIEW

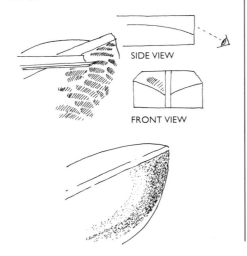

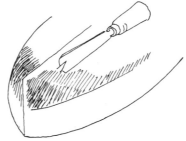

7 Turn the board around and carve the stern, fairing it with a slight curve from the bottom of the boat to the sharp turn in the sides at the back of the boat.

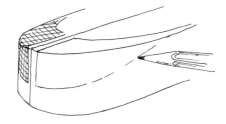

8 Keep well clear of the keel (pencilled in in the illustration) as you work down. Then repeat the procedure on the opposite side.

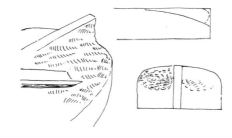

9 Use a flat chisel to define the sides of the keel and rudder.

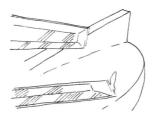

10 Turn the board around again, and cut off the sharp corner of the bow and round it with the flat chisel.

Redraw the centre line and, with the No 8 gouge, carve away the surplus wood to fair the hull to the new shape.

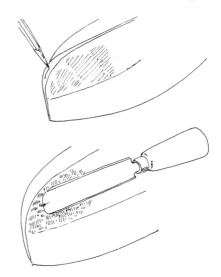

11 Pencil in the rudder at the stern and cut out its shape with a fretsaw or coping saw.

12 Draw in the centre line down the rudder. Round the back edge of the rudder with a flat chisel.

13 Use the No 4 gouge to remove all the ridges between the grooves made by the smaller gouge. Then sand the hull with 60-grit sandpaper backed by a polyethylene-foam block.

Remove the hull from the carving board and mark in the sheerline by hand.

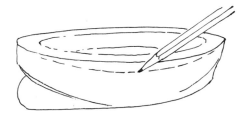

14 The sheerline dips down in the centre of the boat by about ½in (12mm), and if you hold a pencil as shown in the illustration, you will find it easy to control its line relative to the side of the boat.

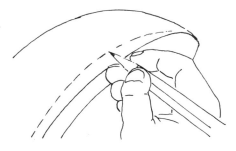

15 Hold the hull lightly in the vice, supporting its floor with a block of wood if necessary, and chisel down to the sheerline. If you work from the ends towards the centre, you will find this is not at all difficult.

When you have defined the sheerline on both sides, chisel away any waste wood remaining proud of the sheerline inside the hull. Invert the hull, lay coarse sandpaper on an offcut of ¾₆in (4mm) plywood, rest the centre of the plywood

on a strip of pine and rub flat the top sheerline of the hull.

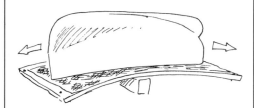

16 If you study the plans, or the photograph on pages 76-7, you will notice that from amidships aft the sides of the hull slope inwards. Carve this feature – known as the 'tumblehome' – by cutting downwards onto a flat board. Make sure that your carving leaves the deck plan symmetrical and that the angles of slope are about the same on both sides.

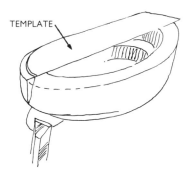
TEMPLATE

17 Using the No 8 gouge, lighten the hull by trimming away excess wood as illustrated. Paint the inside of the hull with a coat of epoxy resin or paint before glueing on the deck.

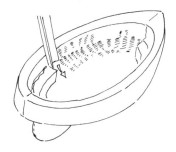

18 Cut the ¾₆in (4mm) plywood deck roughly to shape, coat with epoxy resin the underside of the deck and the top of the hull and press the deck into position. Nail down the edge of the deck with veneer or gimp pins. Trim the edges of the deck when the glue has hardened.

The remaining fitting-out work is easy. The sequence of work is outlined here, and the page references indicate where help with a particular technique can be found.

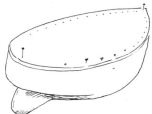

DECKHOUSE

19 Draw the plan of the deckhouse (using a half-plan template if necessary) on 1in (25mm) pine offcut. Mark in the inside line also. Cut around the outline with a jigsaw. Plane and sand it smooth, and drill all the portholes with a brad-point drill.

Finally, hold the deckhouse in the vice and cut around the inside line. Cutting out the inside of the deckhouse after drilling the portholes eliminates the likelihood of splintering the inside walls during drilling.

20 Trim the underside of the deckhouse by holding 60-grit paper face upwards on the deck and grind the deckhouse across the paper until the high point at the front has been sanded down and the deckhouse sits snugly against the deck. Glue the deckhouse to the deck and use the surplus epoxy resin to coat the inside of the deckhouse and the sides of the portholes.

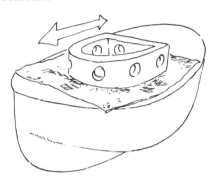

21 Cut out the roof of the deckhouse and round its edges, then mark the hatchway. Make a small hole in one corner of the hatchway with a bradawl or $\frac{1}{16}$in (2mm) drill and saw out the waste with a fretsaw *(see pages 127-8)*. Keep the waste piece. Trim a new hatch cover to shape and size, shaping its top as illustrated. Glue the hatch cover to the waste piece.

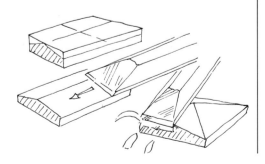

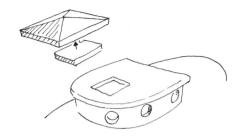

HANDRAILS

22 Cut these from a strip of hardwood. Remove the rough edges at the handholds before glueing and pinning them to the cabin roof.

VENTILATION COWL

23 Carve this from a block of pine or hardwood. The illustrations show the order for doing this. Use a sharp penknife for the fine radius work around the mouth of the cowl. To finish the cowl, hold it in the vice, and with a sharp gouge used in a sideways and slightly circular motion, slice out a depression in its mouth. Use a scrap of sandpaper to remove the ridges left by the carving.

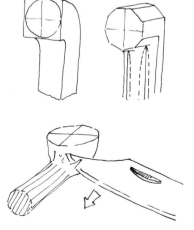

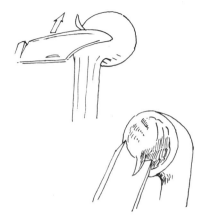

FUNNEL

24 Steady the hull by tacking two straight strips to its bottom. Use the pillar drill fitted with a $\frac{1}{4}$in (6mm) brad-point drill to bore a hole for the mounting dowel through the deckhouse roof and through the deck. Cut and glue a dowel into this hole, leaving it to protrude by $\frac{1}{2}$in (12mm).

Bore a hole in a piece of timber suitable for the funnel and lower the funnel over the dowel. Trim away the funnel's lower edge with a sharp gouge until it sits neatly on the cabin roof. Plane off the hard corners, working around and continually planing until the funnel is a smooth oval in section which requires only sandpapering and finishing.

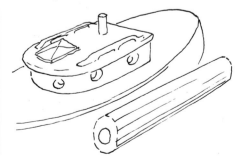

STERN RAILS

25 Cut the stern rails from an offcut of hardwood. They follow the curve of the deck, which means that you

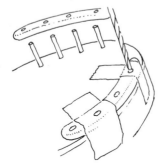

can use the template to find their shape. Sandpaper them smooth, then tape or glue them to the stern deck with superglue. Mark and drill right through the rails into the deck for the post holes. Remove the rails, fit the posts and then glue the rails onto them.

SAMPSON POST AND RUDDER POST

26 Drill right through the deck into the bottom of the hull for the sampson post. Drill the horizontal hole

in the sampson post and fit the cross piece before glueing the post in position. Cut the steering tiller from a small offcut of hardwood. Trim the offcut to size before sawing the curved side section with a fretsaw. On the resulting curved and tapered strip, mark the sides of the tiller and chisel them to the line. Sandpaper the tiller and fretsaw out the slot for the rudder post.

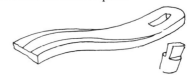

CARVING A SAILOR

The sailor in the photograph on pages 76-7 is carved from cherrywood. If you are going to attempt some carving, you must use a fairly dense and even-textured wood. Pine or oak will prove unsatisfactory, but well-seasoned beech, sycamore, willow, holly, apple, pear or cherry are the ideal choice.

All you need for carving these small figures is plenty of time and a sharp penknife. It will be a help to have a coping saw with which to rough-cut the sailor to shape. Draw the outline of the sailor on the end of the splinter of wood. Hold the wood in the vice and saw round the outline, keeping close to the lines. Avoid sawing any parts so thin that there is no wood left to carve.

Now start to whittle the man to shape. Gently remove the corners from the clothing and face. Use the penknife, bracing and pressing the blade into the wood with the left thumb, while holding the work in the palm of your left hand.

Once the figure begins to take a recognizable form, pencil in the cuffs, boot tops, hat and coat tails, and define them with the penknife.

Now work back from the tips of the fingers, towards the body. Work from the top of the hat downwards. Carve inwards with the intention of not returning to the parts you have left, as these will have become weaker and less well supported as more wood is carved away. As you carve, concentrate on the form you are trying to create, and the direction of the wood grain. These should be your two obsessions while you are carving.

The illustrations show how some of the details of the face and hands are defined by the knife. Avoid too much detail. This can be painted in with water-based body-colour paints before you varnish the figure.

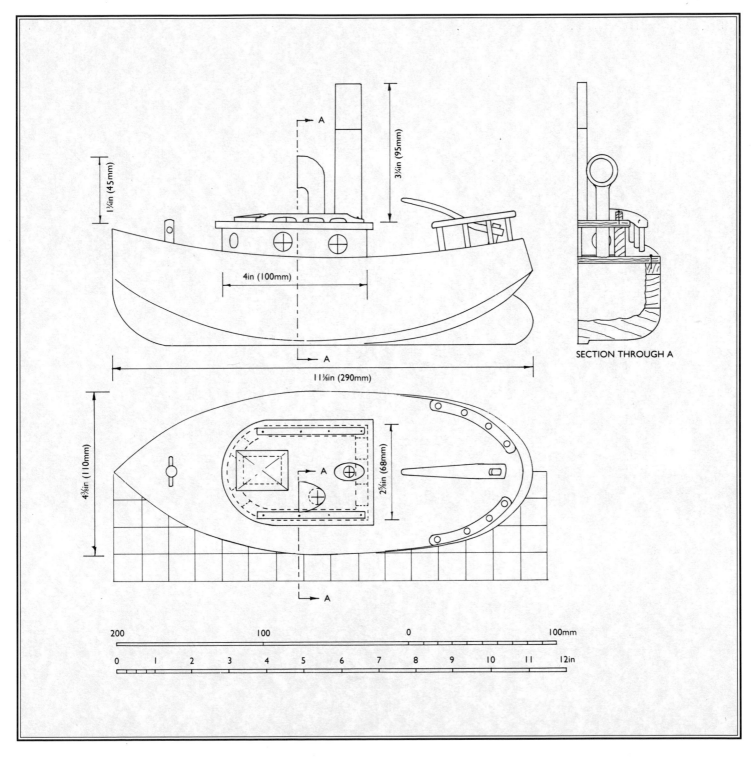

1¾in (45mm)

3¾in (95mm)

4in (100mm)

11⅜in (290mm)

SECTION THROUGH A

A

A

A

A

4⅜in (110mm)

2⅝in (68mm)

200   100   0   100mm

0   1   2   3   4   5   6   7   8   9   10   11   12in

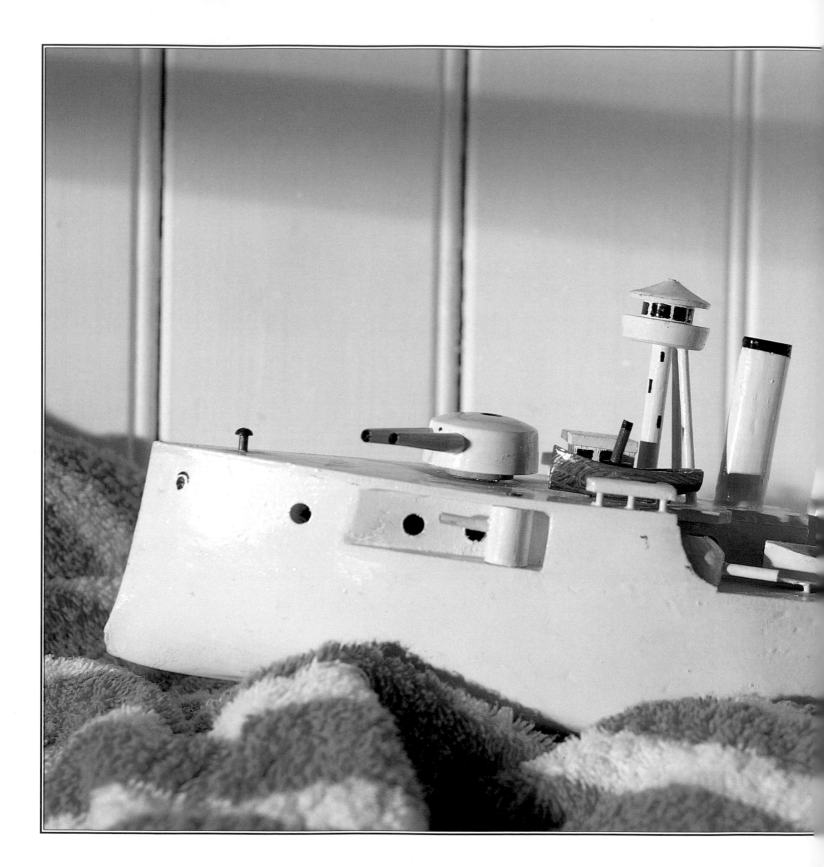

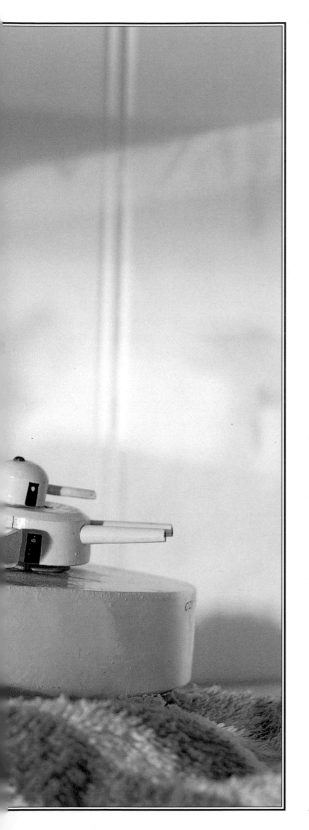

BATTLESHIP

The four big guns carried by this battleship are mounted in circular gun turrets. If you do not have a lathe, you can fit square-sided turrets instead. The biggest turrets are pivoted on dowels which pass through the top decks into the decks below. A 1in (25mm) No 6 countersunk brass screw passes through the top of each turret to anchor the gun in place and allow it to swivel. The smaller gun turrets are made from short lengths of dowel and are pivoted by a single 1in (25mm) No 6 countersunk brass screw.

As with the tugboat and paddle steamer, the battleship's hull is of a sandwich construction, allowing you to create interesting views through the portholes before the decks seal the cabins and prevent access. There are, however, so many details on the decks of this boat that further detailing inside the hull may seem unnecessary.

MATERIALS

¾in x 4in (20mm x 100mm) pine
³⁄₁₆in (4mm) marine plywood
³⁄₁₆in (4mm) dowel
¼in (6mm) dowel
⅜in (9mm) dowel
½in (12mm) dowel
¾in (18mm) dowel
Pine offcuts
Epoxy resin glue

TOOLS

Jigsaw, lathe, pillar drill, gouges:
No 4 (16mm), No 8 (8mm), No 10
(4mm), belt sander and bench-
mounting bracket

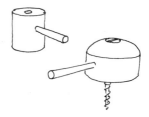 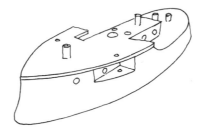

1 Full instructions for building and carving a hull can be found on pages 78-80. Cut the three hull slabs and the two decks. Cut out the centre sections of the two top slabs. Sand and smooth the sides of the top slab where they will be inset from the edges of the hull, and drill the portholes.

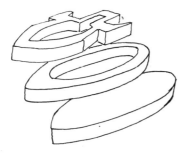

2 Glue the bottom two slabs and the main deck together. Carve the hull shape.

3 Fit the top slab and smooth its sides flush with the hull when the glue has hardened.

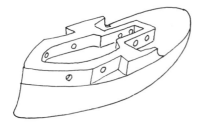

4 Glue the foredeck in position and smooth its sides. Drill ¼in (6mm) holes for the two gun turrets, the gun control tower and the two funnels. Glue the armoured bridge to the top deck.

5 Fretsaw out the two pairs of handrails, tape them to the side deck and drill the post holes.

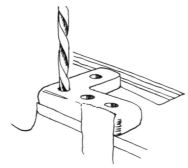

6 Cut the posts and glue the rails in position. Fit the steps to the foredeck.

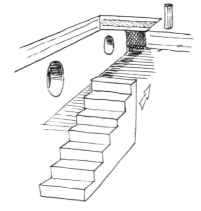

7 Make the small gun turrets. *(For advice on cutting and drilling dowels see page 14.)*

Fit the small turrets, holding them in place with 1in (25mm) No 6 brass countersunk screws.

8 Turn the larger turrets. *(For instructions on turning turrets see page 138.)* Drill the centre hole for the ¼in (6mm) pivot and the shank hole for the No 6 securing screw in each turret.

Fit and glue the dowels which locate the main turrets and the funnels. Lightly bevel their top edges with a penknife.

Turn the gun platform (make it rectangular or hexagonal if you do not have a lathe), drill its base for the three holes and glue it to the top of the main mast.

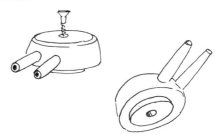

9 Drill two ³⁄₁₆in (4mm) holes for the control tower supports, and then with the tower and mast in position, estimate their length and cut and fit them.

Shape and fit the funnels.

Carve the launches and lifeboats and fit them to the deck with two short lengths of ¹⁄₁₆in (2mm) dowel. *(For instructions on carving the very small boats see page 87.)*

The battleship is now ready for painting. Remove the boats and turrets before painting the hull and decks.

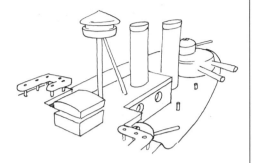

CARVING SMALL BOATS

10 The only problem in carving small boats from soft wood is that it is difficult to hollow them out once the hull shape has been carved. They are too small and delicate to fit in the vice, and it is unsafe to hold them in your hand while wielding a gouge with the other.

11 To make these boats, first define their outline with a cardboard or paper template on a length of square-section softwood. Then carve out the inside of the boat, using the outline as a guide.

12 Now place in the vice the length of wood that your boat has been marked on, with the boat's end hanging over the side. Use a ¼in (6mm) straight chisel to carve the midship and stern sections.

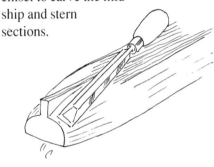

13 Trim the stern and then saw off the boat at the bow. Whittle the bow to shape with a penknife.

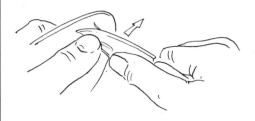

14 The seats, boilers, funnels and other features are carved with a penknife and glued in place when the hull is finished.

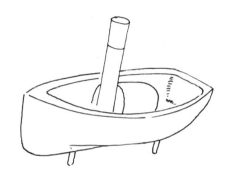

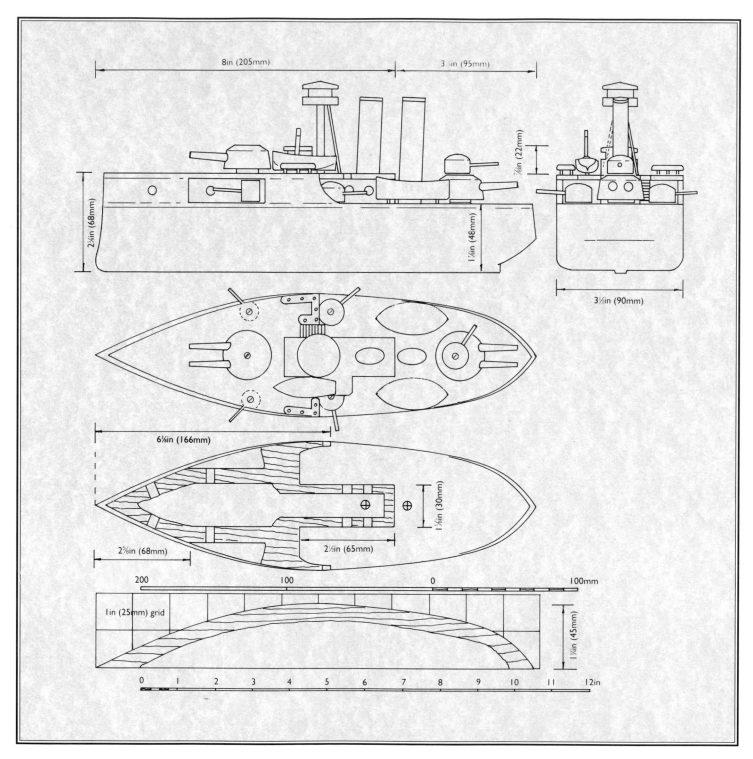

8in (205mm)

3¾in (95mm)

⅞in (22mm)

2⅝in (68mm)

1⅞in (48mm)

3½in (90mm)

6½in (166mm)

1⅛in (30mm)

2⅝in (68mm)

2½in (65mm)

200   100   0   100mm

1in (25mm) grid

1¾in (45mm)

0   1   2   3   4   5   6   7   8   9   10   11   12in

WOOD

Most of the toys described in this book are made from softwood obtainable from a builder's merchant. In general, the pieces needed to make these toys are so small that you need not worry about twists in the wood, or knots. It is more important that the surfaces of the wood are clean, square with each other and smooth.

Wood that has been stored outside is likely to have a higher moisture content than is desirable. Bring the pieces you plan to use indoors to dry out, one or two days before you start work on them.

The toys can be made from hardwood, and some of them should be. Do not buy equatorial hardwoods. Unless they are high-quality, expensive timbers (such as Honduran or Brazilian mahogany), they will not be pleasant to handle, and will not look special. In addition, you may be supporting a trade in illegal hardwoods that is detrimental to the lives of the people who live in those regions from which the wood comes.

Instead, you can obtain your hardwood supplies from one of the woodyards which can be found in the outskirts of most large towns and, more commonly, in the country. Buy wood that is not in great demand. For example, alder, poplar, chestnut, willow, apple, birch and beech are all handsome and beautiful woods to work, and cheap. Cedar of Lebanon is another lovely wood to work, but it is oily, and apt to spoil its paint finish. Seek advice from the woodyard's foreman, who will be able to tell you whether the wood is suitable, and sufficiently seasoned. He may well be able to plane it for you as well. Small local woodyards are often happy to sell at a discount offcuts from larger orders.

For those who are not familiar with woodworking, the following illustrations show how the direction of the grain affects the strength and handling qualities of wood.

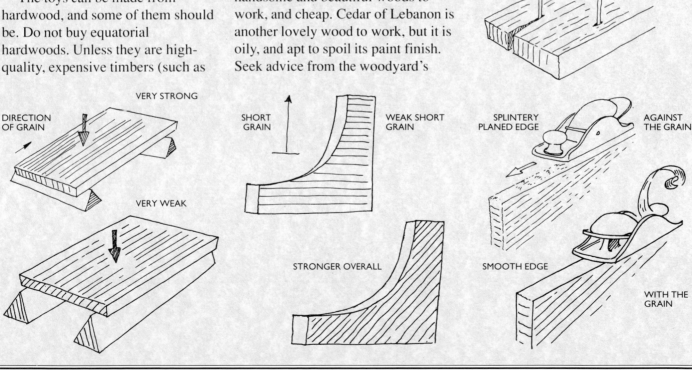

WEAK SHORT GRAIN – SPLITS UNLESS NAIL IS PRE-DRILLED

LONG GRAIN – NAIL WILL NOT SPLIT WOOD ACROSS THE GRAIN

VERY STRONG

DIRECTION OF GRAIN

VERY WEAK

SHORT GRAIN

WEAK SHORT GRAIN

STRONGER OVERALL

SPLINTERY PLANED EDGE

AGAINST THE GRAIN

SMOOTH EDGE

WITH THE GRAIN

PADDLE STEAMER

The stern-wheeler described here is a copy of a small wooden toy made by my grandfather for his family. It is designed to take advantage of a unique drive system. The stern paddle-wheel is turned by a belt powered by a long double strip of elastic which hooks onto a crank at the masthead and onto the drive wheel at the foot of the mast. The elastic is wound up by turning the crank at the masthead while holding the main drive wheel stationary. When the drive wheel is released, the elastic spins the paddles and the boat is moved forward. A surprising secondary effect of the high-speed paddle is that it ladles water into the hull. In my revised version, the stern is raised and the drive belt passes through a diagonal slot in the transom. This modification makes it possible for the boat to be fitted with a light deck and super-structure.

MATERIALS

1⅜in x 5in (35mm x 125mm) pine
¼in (6mm) dowel
Pine and ¼in (6mm) and ³⁄₁₆in (4mm)
  marine plywood offcuts
Model aeroplane propeller elastic
Short length of 16-gauge copper or
  galvanized wire
Two small glass beads
Epoxy resin glue

TOOLS

Jigsaw, lathe, pillar drill, gouges:
No 4 (16mm), No 8 (8mm), No 10
(4mm)

1 Make a template of the hull shape from the plans, cut out the two slabs and remove the waste section from the centre of the upper slab with a jigsaw.

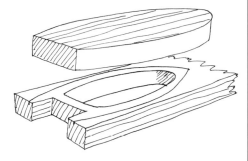

2 Glue the slabs together with epoxy resin glue, then carve the outside hull to shape using the techniques described on pages 78-80. When the outside of the hull is finished, release it from the carving board.

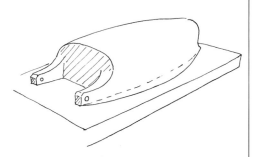

3 Place the hull in the vice, resting it on a block which lifts it partially out of the vice, and clamp it tight. Smooth the sides and ends of the inside of the

hull with a No 8 and then a No 4 gouge, and remove some of the excess wood in the bottom of the hull at the same time.

4 In this slightly awkward position, it will not be possible to remove a clean shaving with each pass of the gouge, and two cuts will usually be needed to remove each shaving. The first is a scooping cut along the grain, working from one end of the boat, while the second releases the shaving with an angled or vertical incision.

5 As you become familiar with this simple technique, you can carve small, neat shavings down the grain, towards the back of the boat, and remove them with a chisel, which will finish the flat transom on the inside. Be careful not to make the sides or bottom less than ⅜in (9mm) thick. As your work nears completion, periodically remove the hull from the vice and check its thickness with your thumb and forefinger.

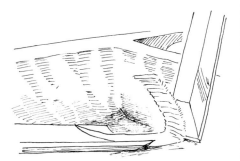

6 Now drill the holes in the ends of the beam which overhang the stern for the wire paddle-wheel axle.

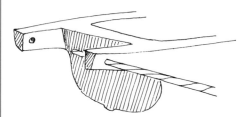

7 Fit the small plywood deck which holds the mast and drive wheel. The easiest way to do this is to make a cardboard template of the deck and use it to mark off the shape on the plywood.

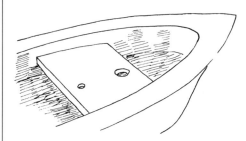

8 Drill the deck for the mast and the main wire bearing and then glue it in position. For additional security, two thin battens are trimmed and glued between the sides and the deck to prevent the deck pulling out.

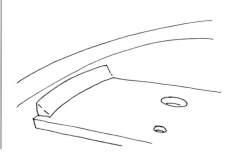

9 Use the pillar drill to drill the housing hole for the main bearing in the bottom of the boat.

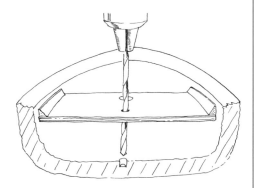

10 Fit the ¼in (6mm) dowel for the mast, through the hole in the deck. Holding the tip of the mast in its correct position over the bearing hole, mark on the floor of the boat the position for the mast step hole, which you can now drill.

11 Draw the masthead fitting onto a scrap of ¼in (6mm) plywood, drill it for the crank bearing and the masthead and then cut it to shape with a fretsaw. Glue the masthead fitting to the top of the mast, leaving the mast protruding by no more than ¹⁄₁₆in (2mm). Use a penknife to cut into the mast the top groove, which will hold the crank when the elastic is wound tight.

12 The rear paddle is easily made. It does not need to be turned, but can be made from a piece of cork, balsa wood or solid pine. Drill an oversize hole through its centre to allow the paddle-wheel to rotate freely, and mark and drill ¼in (6mm) holes around its sides to hold the paddles. Carve the paddles from a pine offcut strip of ½in x ¼in (12mm x 6mm) in section, more or less in the shape shown. Check the length of the paddles before glueing the ends into the paddle-wheel.

STAGES IN CARVING THE PADDLES

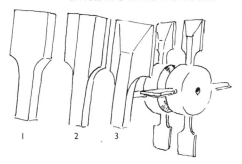

13 The main drive wheel can either be turned or built up from three discs of plywood. The centre disc should have a smaller diameter than the other two and the rims of the outer pair should be chamfered and smoothed.

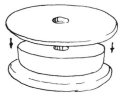

Select the bearing wire. The bottom end of the bearing sits in the recess in the hull, where it can turn freely. At the top end the wire is formed into a loop, the end of which returns into the top of the main drive wheel, where it is secured in place with a drop of epoxy resin.

14 The main bearing wire is prevented from pulling out of the deck by a short length of thin copper or galvanized wire which passes through a hole in the bearing wire below the deck, and then is wound around the bearing wire as illustrated. The two glass beads act as a thrust bearing between the thin wire and the deck.

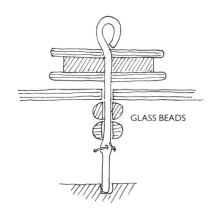

GLASS BEADS

15 Take a short length of copper or galvanized bearing wire and rest it on a block of iron. Use the back of a pin hammer to tap a very small flat in the wire, about 1in (25mm) up from its end. Centrepunch a mark in the centre of the flat and then drill through the wire with a fine drill. When this is done, all that remains to do is to complete the loop at the top of the bearing wire and slip the ends into the drive wheel. Because of the slight thickening of the wire, it may be necessary to enlarge the hole in the deck before you can fit the main bearing wire into position.

16 Fit the drive belt around the pulley and slip it over the main drive wheel. Mark on the stern the positions of the belt where it passes across the stern, and saw a slot which allows the belt to run straight to the paddle and back without obstruction.

Remove the belt and sandpaper the slot smooth before painting the hull.

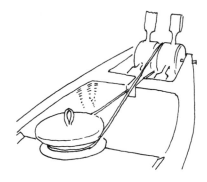

17 Assemble the propulsion system after the boat has been painted. First, fit the main bearing wire and drive wheel assembly. Poke the point of the wire through the hole in the deck, slip on the two glass beads and then twist the thin copper wire through the bearing wire and around it a few times to prevent the lower bead from pulling through. Next slip the drive belt over the centre of the paddle-wheel and fit the paddle-wheel in position. Now pull one end of the aeroplane propeller elastic through the loop in the top of the main drive wheel, take it up through the hook in the wire crank at the masthead and tie the ends of the elastic together.

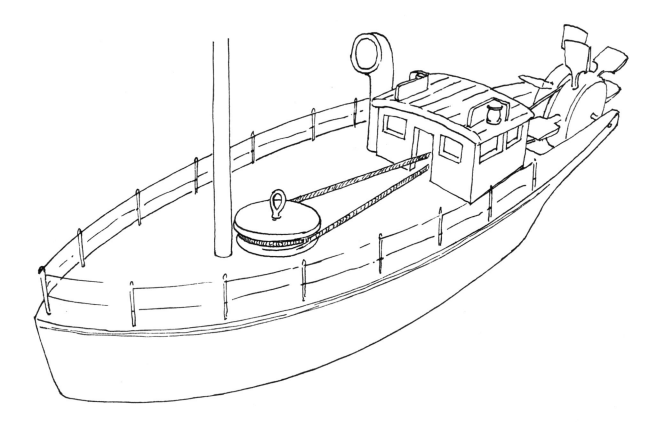

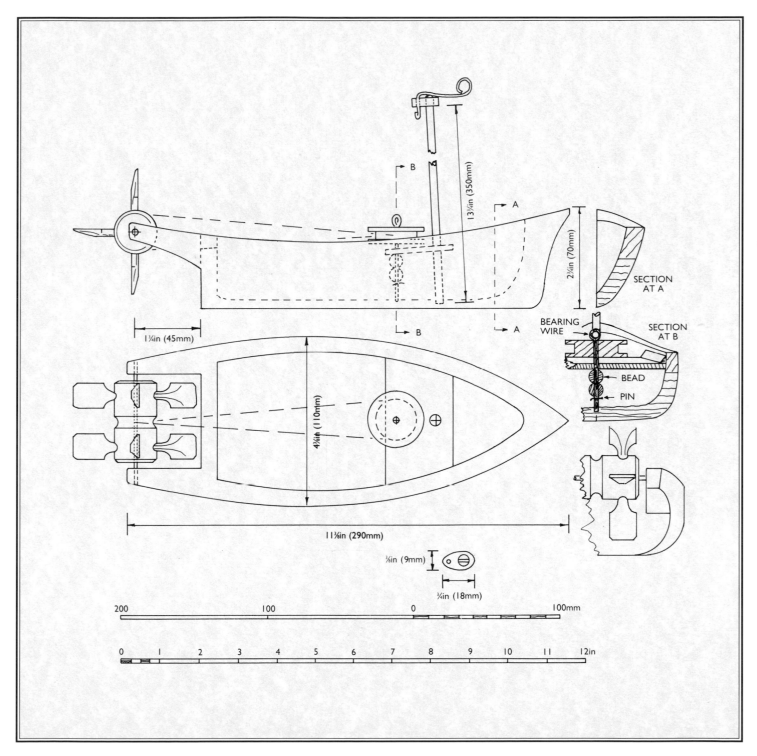

13¾in (350mm)

1¾in (45mm)

B

B

A

A

SECTION
AT A

2¾in (70mm)

BEARING
WIRE

SECTION
AT B

BEAD

PIN

4⅜in (110mm)

11⅜in (290mm)

⅜in (9mm)

¾in (18mm)

200   100   0   100mm

0   1   2   3   4   5   6   7   8   9   10   11   12in

TOYS TO
SIT ON

CARVED HORSE

If you are planning to give this wooden horse as a present, allow yourself plenty of time to carve it. Even with the large No 10 gouge, there will be a lot of wood to remove before you find your horse. You should buy ready-planed timber, preferably a single piece, and cut it into lengths as specified below, to minimize variation in moisture content between the blocks which are glued together to make the horse.

It is a daunting prospect to be faced with a vast, hard-edged block of wood, in the knowledge that everyone expects you to make a horse from it. The most important thing to remember is that you are not actually making the horse at all: what you are doing is cutting away those bits which are not the horse. Work gently and concentrate on the feel and the appearance of the animal, removing thin layers of waste and eliminating hard corners, until you find the ears, neck and so on.

If some unkind person remarks that what you are carving resembles a cross between a monkey and a hippopotamus, you should not feel insulted. Those animals are there too.

MATERIALS

2 x 8ft x 6½in x 1⅜in (2400mm x 165mm x 35mm) planed, knot-free pine or any other easily carved wood
4 x 2½in (65mm) No 10 counter-sunk steel screws
Unused cotton mop head
Epoxy resin glue and colloidal silica thickeners

TOOLS

Jigsaw, pillar drill, carving gouges: No 4 (16mm), No 8 (8mm), No 10 (4mm), large No 10 (30mm), No 11 (6mm)

1 The horse rests on a simple thick plank. At each end a rod passes through the plank. The ends of the rods form the axles. Square off the base with a set square and mark in the locations for the axles. Square down the sides of the plank from the axle line and mark the centre for each hole.

Because of its width, the plank has to be drilled from both sides. Ask a friend to sight the vertical plane of the drill bit while you hold the drill and sight the horizontal plane from above. If the drill is not long enough to reach the centre, drill the second pair of holes and then hammer a crude cutter to the end of one of the axle rods, clamp it in the drill chuck and finish the connecting hole with that.

The wheels are plain, cut with a jigsaw and then sanded smooth. The hole should be in the middle, but the wheels themselves need not be perfectly round. There is an advantage in imperfect wheels, since irregularities in the perimeters of the wheels will tend to slow the horse down. It will move easily enough, but it will not roll so fast and is slightly less likely to damage furniture in its way.

Do not fit the wheels and axles at this stage. The base itself will serve as a carving board until the horse is finished.

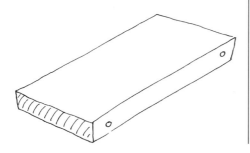

JOINING BLOCKS TO MAKE A HORSE

2 Make a template of the profile of the horse. You will have to reproduce full-size the grid marked on the plans. Then, taking a square at a time, mark on the full-sized grid the points where the curved profile of the horse intersect with the grid. Join the marks free hand and cut out the profile.

Set aside two blocks and taking each remaining block in turn, place the template over it. Ensure that the base of the block and the template align, and draw around the edge of the template. Saw around the pencil lines with the jigsaw and stack the four shaped pieces together.

Mark on the template the new base line for the second tier of wood. Take the other two uncut blocks, place the template on one, arrange the new base line to coincide with the bottom of the block and draw around the template. Repeat this four times, using both ends of each block for this part of the horse. The remaining offcuts can be marked and cut to shape to form the top of the head and the ears.

Since all of these pieces are already planed square and are the same width, they can be assembled in a stack and glued together. Before glueing, roughen the surfaces with a spare hacksaw blade to increase the penetration of the resin into the wood fibres.

When you mix and work with epoxy resin in a large quantity, the heat generated during hardening has a tendency to accelerate the reaction, generating further heat. Once this

exothermic reaction gets out of control, the epoxy in your mixing tub will become very hot, and harden far more quickly than you can use it. To prevent this happening, mix the resin in a wide tub and mix the minimum quantity necessary at a time.

In this case, the four profiles can be glued together in pairs and the two sides can be joined together in a third glueing operation. Collect the components for the two left-hand-side profiles, mark the centre surface and lay the blocks in position, centre-side downwards, on a flat board protected by a sheet of polythene.

Mix together what you estimate to be a little more than enough epoxy resin to glue the two profiles together, and add the colloidal thickeners. Assemble the pieces with plenty of glue between them, stack one profile on top of the other, cover them with clear polythene and rest weights on top. There is no mechanical or other advantage in using clamps to hold the pieces together.

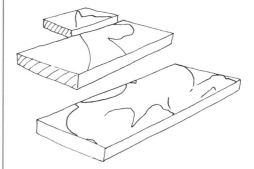

3 Now glue together the second pair of profiles. The centre face of this pair must be face downwards on the flat board so that the two halves of the horse will fit together perfectly. Then, in a third operation, glue the two sides together to form the horse. When the glue has hardened, plane the underside of the horse flat.

Carve the horse on a carving board, bolted to the workbench by a central ⅜in (9mm) coach bolt. This will enable you to alter the position of the carving when you need to.

The base itself makes an excellent carving board, provided its top surface is protected by a sheet of scrap plywood or MDF. Cut a suitable board to fit over the top of the base and then drill a ⅜in (9mm) hole through the centre of them both. Enlarge the hole in the protective board so that the head of the coach bolt is below the surface.

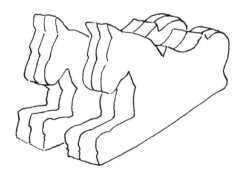

4 Pin the board to the base with a couple of veneer pins and, with the bolt and horse block in position, screw the underside of the horse to the top of the block, using four 2½in (65mm) No 10 steel countersunk screws. Two screws hold the front hooves and two hold the horse at the back end.

Now fit the bolt through a suitable hole in the bench and draw a centre line down the back, neck, head and chest of the horse. Mark in the width of the front

legs and start the carving. First remove the hard corners of the block, then shape the saddle. From the saddle, work up the neck, shaping and tapering it as you work upwards.

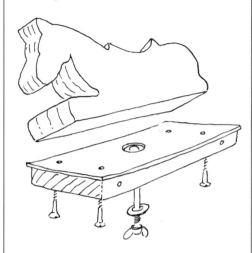

5 The direction of the wood grain is consistent throughout the horse, and therefore you will be able to work quickly, hitting the gouge smartly with a woodcarver's mallet. *(For advice on using chisels and gouges and sharpening them see pages 129-31.)*

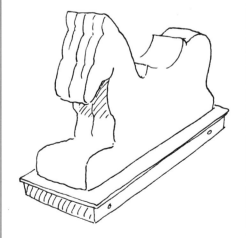

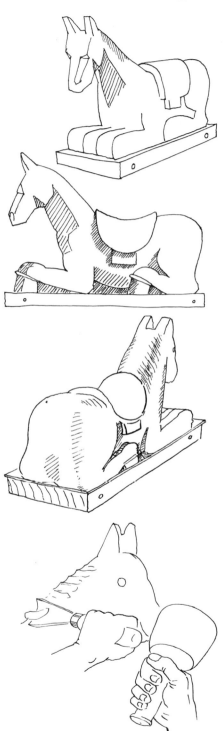

6 The illustrations above suggest some of the stages which your horse might experience as it is carved. Remember never to undercut a feature unless it is absolutely essential, and then only at the very end of the carving. Undercutting tends to weaken a carving both physically and aesthetically, and the example I have used is the saddle flap, which should not be undermined. If it is, the sharp prominent edge is left vulnerable and looks weak.

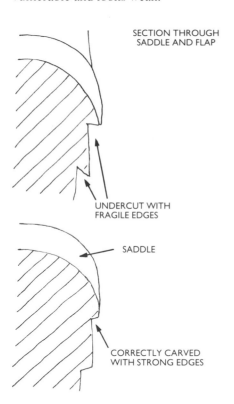

SECTION THROUGH SADDLE AND FLAP

UNDERCUT WITH FRAGILE EDGES

SADDLE

CORRECTLY CARVED WITH STRONG EDGES

7 The front legs are, of course, undercut, but only after the shaping of the upper leg is complete. Imagine how sad it would be to have undercut the leg, only to find out later that there is no wood left with which to correct your mistakes.

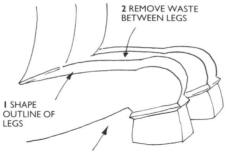

2 REMOVE WASTE BETWEEN LEGS

1 SHAPE OUTLINE OF LEGS

3 DEFINE AND CARVE UNDERSIDE OF LEG ONCE THE SHAPING OF THE UPPER SURFACES IS COMPLETE

8 The following drawings, which incorporate sections of the finished features, are to help with the detailing.

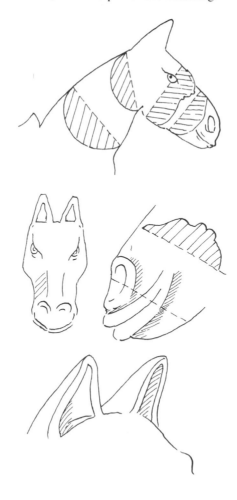

They are only suggestions, and you may want to stop the carving before you reach this level of detail, or you may want to spend more time refining the carving still further.

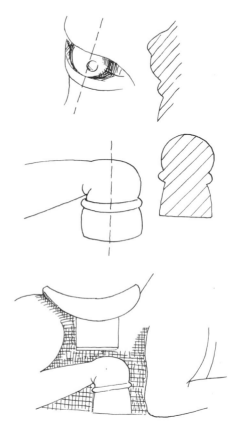

9 Rasp and sandpaper the carving smooth before removing the horse from the base, then finish the shaping and smoothing at the hooves and under the forelegs. Stain the horse before you fix it back onto the board. The horse in the photograph on pages 98-9 was stained with two coats of methylated-spirits-soluble black aniline dye. The dye was brushed on with a house-painter's 2in (50mm) brush and, because of the variations in grain pattern, was

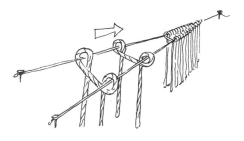

absorbed quite unevenly. Care was taken to avoid letting the dye stain the saddle, or the eyes, which were dyed with a brown oak aniline dye, as were the mounting board and wheels. Each coat takes about 20 minutes to dry. Leave the horse for at least an hour before you varnish it by applying a diluted coat of urethane varnish.

As you can tell from the photograph, no attempt has been made to conceal the joins in the blocks forming the body of the horse. To do this, it would have been necessary to fill all the cracks in the horse, sand it again and then apply a commercial brand of grain filler. After filling, and wiping away the unused grain filler, I would have stained the horse, and then varnished it with several coats of undiluted varnish, and rubbed the penultimate coat smooth with 220-grit paper before finishing. When using a high-build urethane varnish, allow plenty of time for the varnish to dry. Treat the drying times marked on the cans as minimum times.

Fit the wheels onto their axles, and then screw the horse back onto its mounting board.

TAIL

10 Drill a ¾in (18mm) hole into the backside of the horse, just below the saddle. Take strands from the mop head, cotton rope or whatever you want to use for the tail, and whip the ends together with a series of thumb knots on alternate sides to form the whipping.

Soak the whipped end of the tail in PVA glue. Cut and stain a wedge, semicircular in section, press the tail

into the hole and drive in the wedge to hold it. The wedge should be fitted under the tail, which then conceals it.

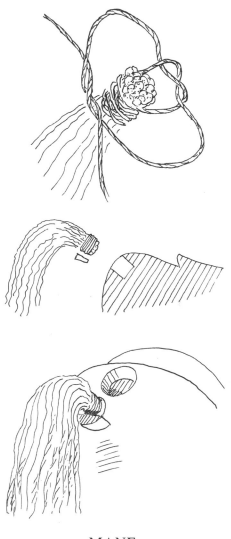

MANE

11 The mane is made from short strands from the mop head, woven between two lengths of line. Each strand is knotted as shown, and pushed up hard against the previous strands, which should all hang downwards.

12 Use a length of woven strands equal to twice the length of the mane. Once you have made up enough mane, sew the ends of the line together and glue and staple the mane in place.

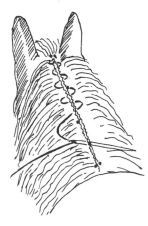

13 When the mane is tacked in place, sew the two strings of mane together, and brush them down each side of the neck and over the brow. Trim the mane with scissors.

GRID:
20mm = 50mm
¾in = 2in

STEAM TRAIN

The central pair of large-diameter driving wheels, linked by connecting rods, is located in slots in the chassis of the train, so they do not carry any weight unless the train passes over a steep bump. The front bogie is turned by a continuous chain which passes beneath the main wheel mounts and is anchored to a drum at the base of the steering column. Turning the steering column winds one side of the chain loop onto the drum and unwinds the other side from it.

At the front of the locomotive, the chain passes around and is stapled to a circular wheel, which also doubles as the outer ring of the front steering bearing. The purpose of this ring is to bear the brunt of the horizontal forces applied to the front wheels as the train rolls along, preventing bending of the ¼in (6mm) coach bolt holding the front bogie to the chassis.

All of the techniques used in building this toy are described elsewhere in the book, so the instructions here concentrate primarily on the order of construction.

MATERIALS

¾in x 9in (18mm x 220mm) pine
2in x 1½in (50mm x 40mm) pine
¾in x 5in (18mm x 125mm) pine or
  plywood for wheels
¼in (6mm) birch-faced plywood
¼in (6mm) steel rod
¼in (6mm) dowel
Brass chain
3in x ¼in (75mm x 6mm) coach bolt
Pine offcuts for funnel, pressure
  dome, steeering wheel
2 x 2¼in (55mm) brass hinges

TOOLS

Jigsaw, lathe, power drill, tank
cutter

1 Cut out the main chassis plank. Square the ends and cut out the two recesses in each side. Mark and drill the ¼in (6mm) hole for the front steering bolt.

Make a template for the cabin sides and cut them from a wide board. Tack the two boards together and smooth their edges. Trim a board to the exact width of the cabin front and use the same circular saw setting to cut to length the boards at the front and back of the tender.

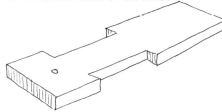

2 Shape the top of the cabin front and drill out the two circular windows with a tank cutter. Mark the exact location of the cabin front on the main chassis plank, and mark and drill the hole for the ¼in (6mm) steel steering column.

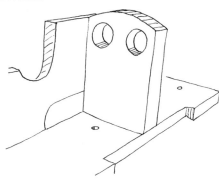

3 Glue and nail the front of the cabin in place. Glue and nail one cabin side to the chassis and to the cabin front. Punch the heads of the nails below the surface of the wood.

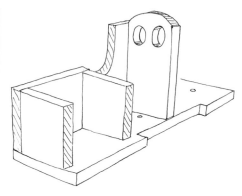

4 Nail and glue both ends of the tender to the side and chassis. Glue and nail the second cabin side to the chassis, the cabin front and the two ends of the tender. Punch the nail heads below the surfaces of the wood and fill the holes with a two-part wood filler.

Trim the top of the tender level with a block plane.

Fit the two side blocks at the floor of the cabin and glue them.

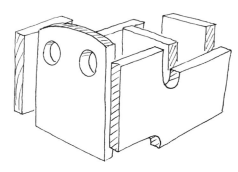

5 Cut a plywood board to fit over the blocks and cut a recess at the front

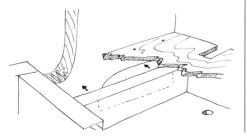

of the board for the steering column. Glue the board in position inside the cabin.

Plane the top edge of the cabin sides flush with the curved top of the cabin front. Make the curved cabin roof from about six pine offcuts.

6 Angle both sides of each pine strip, so that the cabin roof matches the curve of the cabin front. Glue the strips together with PVA glue, holding them tightly in place with masking tape.

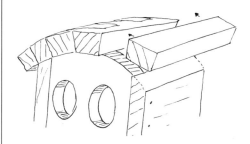

7 Cut out two circles of pine for the ends of the boiler. Trim them on the lathe. Screw and glue a batten between them to hold them square and the correct distance apart.

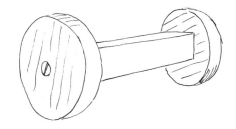

8 Cut out strips for the body of the boiler. Calculate the angle of the bevels needed at the sides of each strip by marking out the outside diameter of the boiler on a piece of paper, dividing

the perimeter into the widths of the strips, and extending the line to the centre point. The angle between the tangential strips and the centre is the angle at which the sides of the strips will have to be planed.

Plane all the strips, then line them up on the workbench and tape them all together. When they are linked together, wrap them around the two circular boiler ends. Adjust the strips until they fit tightly around the ends and touch where they meet.

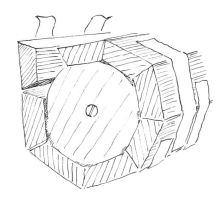

9 Lay the taped-together strips, with their inside faces upwards, on the workbench and allow plenty of PVA glue to run between each strip. Apply more glue to the sides of the boiler ends, and wrap the strips around the ends to form the boiler.

When the glue is dry, remove the masking tape and the screws in the ends of the boiler. Hold the boiler in the vice and plane off the sharp bumps until it is a more or less regular cylinder. Now place the boiler in the lathe and hold the block plane against the side of the boiler while the lathe turns slowly. Finish the smoothing by holding a strip of sandpaper against the boiler. While the

boiler is still between the lathe centres, trim the ends flat.

Cut out the simple block which sits beneath the boiler at the front of the train, and trim its top face so that it fits neatly against the curve of the boiler. Before fitting the boiler to the locomotive, place this block against the cabin face and pencil in the curve of the boiler on the cabin face. This will give an accurate location for the back end of the boiler, which should be parallel with the chassis plank when it rests on its front bearer.

Pencil in the centre line of the cabin, and from the pencil mark left by the bearing block, mark the centre of the boiler. At that point, drill a hole through the cabin front for a No 10 countersunk screw. Countersink the hole on the inside of the cabin face and push the screw through the hole, from inside the cabin.

Glue the back face of the boiler and both glueing faces of the bearer, and wind the boiler onto the screw until it is pressing hard against the cabin face. Lift the boiler slightly and slip the bearer beneath it.

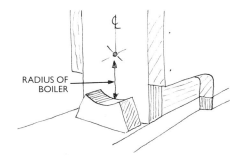

RADIUS OF BOILER

10 Glue the boiler face plate to the front end of the boiler and nail it in place with evenly spaced gimp pins.

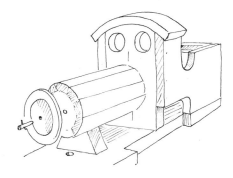

11 Now fit the funnel and pressure dome. The base of the funnel should be 1⅜in (35mm) in diameter, and the bottom of the pressure dome 1¾in (45mm). Use a saw-toothed tank cutter to cut ⅜in (9mm) recesses for the funnel and dome. Chisel away the waste from inside the saw cut, and turn the dome and funnel to fit the holes provided. *(For advice on turning see pages 133-8.)*

Cut out the lid for the tender. This is supported underneath by a pair of wooden battens, and is hinged to the front edge of the tender by two brass cabinet hinges. Fit the two wooden battens on the underside of the lid. They should slip between the sides of the tender, and limit any sideways play. Once they are in position, draw round the sides of the tender, and trim the lid to the line. Plane a radius on the upper two side edges, and then on the ends. Place the hinges in position on the front edge of the lid, and screw them in place.

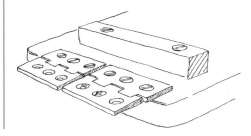

12 Rest the lid back on the tender, and pencil onto the front edge of the tender the exact location of the two hinges.

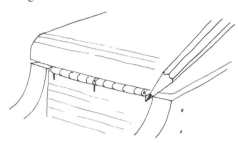

13 Remove the lid and square across the edge, and also scribe a line for the hinge recess with a marking gauge *(see page 131)*. Note that almost the full depth of the hinge will have to be recessed into the edge of the tender, as the upper flap of the hinge is screwed directly onto the lid and is not recessed.

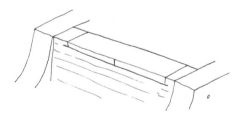

DEPTH OF RECESS

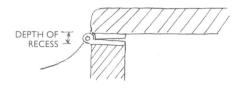

14 Saw down the sides of the hinge marks to the gauge mark. Make several sawcuts between the outer marks to weaken the waste, without sawing beyond the gauge mark. Remove the waste with a sharp ⅝in (15mm) chisel, and fit the lid. The hinges should make a

snug fit in the recess. Screw them in position.

Fit the simple catch at the back of the tender after the engine has been painted.

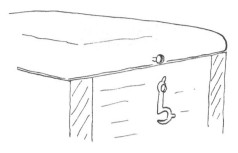

CHASSIS, STEERING MECHANISM AND WHEELS

15 Shape the two main girders that fit below the slots in the chassis. Pin the two girders together, then mark and drill the holes for the chain guide and the ¼in (6mm) holes which define the ends of the axle slots. Use a coping saw, router or fretsaw to cut out the two slots. Smooth their sides with a file.

The axles, which fit in the slots, are held in position by the floating plate between the two girders. This plate holds the two axles in their precise positions relative to each other, permitting the connecting rods screwed to the perimeter of the large wheels to be fitted.

CHAIN GUIDE

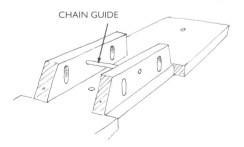

16 The floating plate is made from a small strip of ¼in (6mm) plywood, with a block at each end through which is drilled a ¼in (6mm) hole. Glue the blocks to the board and when the glue is dry, bore the holes in the end blocks with the pillar drill.

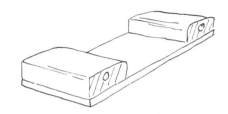

17 Insert the axles, plate and chain guide between the outer girders, and glue and nail the girders to the underside of the chassis. Make certain before nailing the girders to the chassis that the chain plate can move freely up and down inside the slots in the girders. This movement is necessary, because the large diameter wheels have to touch the ground yet should not bear any weight. If they were load-bearing, it would cause the steering to be very difficult to operate.

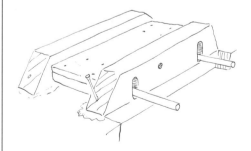

18 Mark and drill the hole in the cabin roof and pass the steering column through the roof and down into the chassis. You can now make and glue

the simple plywood collar which slips round the column and is glued to the cabin floor.

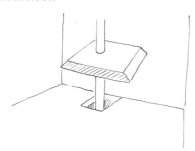

19 The chain drum is made up from two plywood outer discs glued to the top and bottom of a hardwood drum. The drum is pinned to the column and the chain is nailed to the drum.

20 Make the front bogie assembly. *(For advice on turning the rings see page 136.)* Note that the steering pivot bolt is trapped by the outer bearing ring.

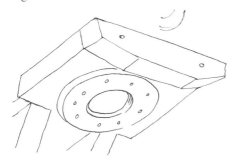

21 Glue and nail the outer bearing ring to the axle block and then fit the inner bearing ring, glueing this over the pivot bolt shaft and nailing through into the top of the axle block.

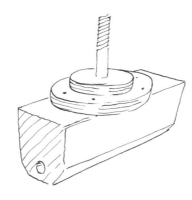

22 Cut the rear axle block and support assembly. Drill the axle holes through the tapered supports and mark and drill the main block with a ⅜in (9mm) drill bit. Glue the unit together, after glueing and nailing the plywood plate to the axle block.

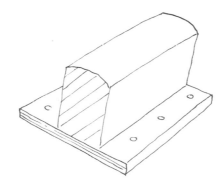

23 When the plywood plate is glued and nailed to the bottom of the train chassis plate, fit the tapered supports. These are pre-drilled and glued in place. First clamp them against the axle block and nail them into the

chassis plate, and then after the clamp is released nail them into the axle block.

Wait until the glue has dried before marking and drilling the axle holes in the tapered supports.

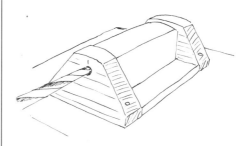

24 The wheels are turned as described on page 134. The steering wheel is turned from a pine board, backed by a sheet of plywood. The tapered collar beneath the wheel is glued beneath the steering wheel, and the steering column is pinned through the collar in exactly the same way that the drum is pinned to the base of the column.

Assemble the wheels, connecting rods and steering chain after the train has been painted.

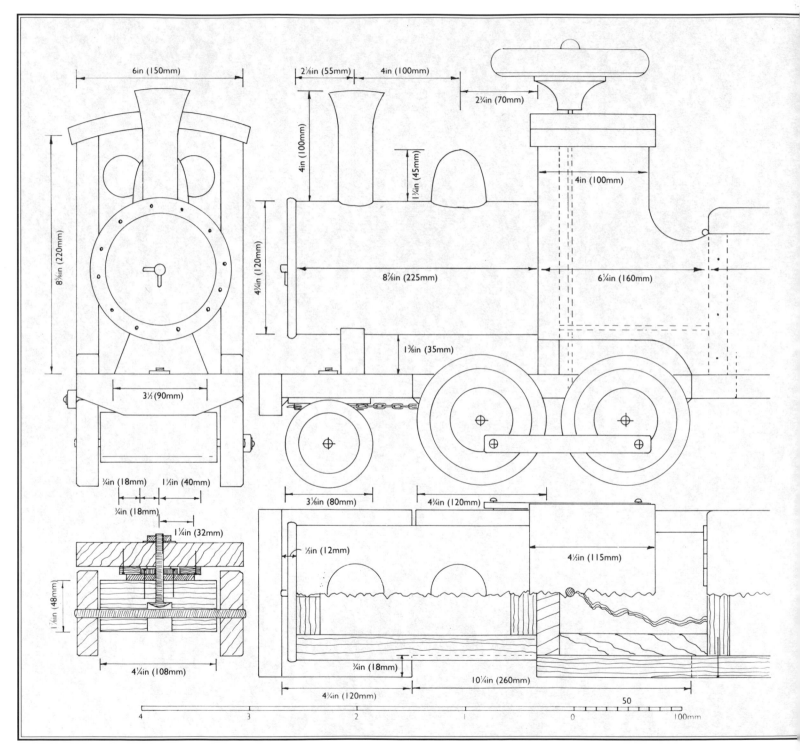

6in (150mm)

2⅛in (55mm) 4in (100mm)

2¾in (70mm)

4in (100mm)

4in (100mm)

1¾in (45mm)

8⅝in (220mm)

4¾in (120mm)

8⅞in (225mm)

6¼in (160mm)

1⅜in (35mm)

3½ (90mm)

¾in (18mm) 1½in (40mm)

3⅛in (80mm) 4¾in (120mm)

¾in (18mm)

1¼in (32mm)

½in (12mm)

4½in (115mm)

1⅞in (48mm)

4¼in (108mm)

¾in (18mm)

10¼in (260mm)

4¾in (120mm)

50

4   3   2   1   0   100mm

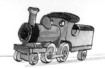

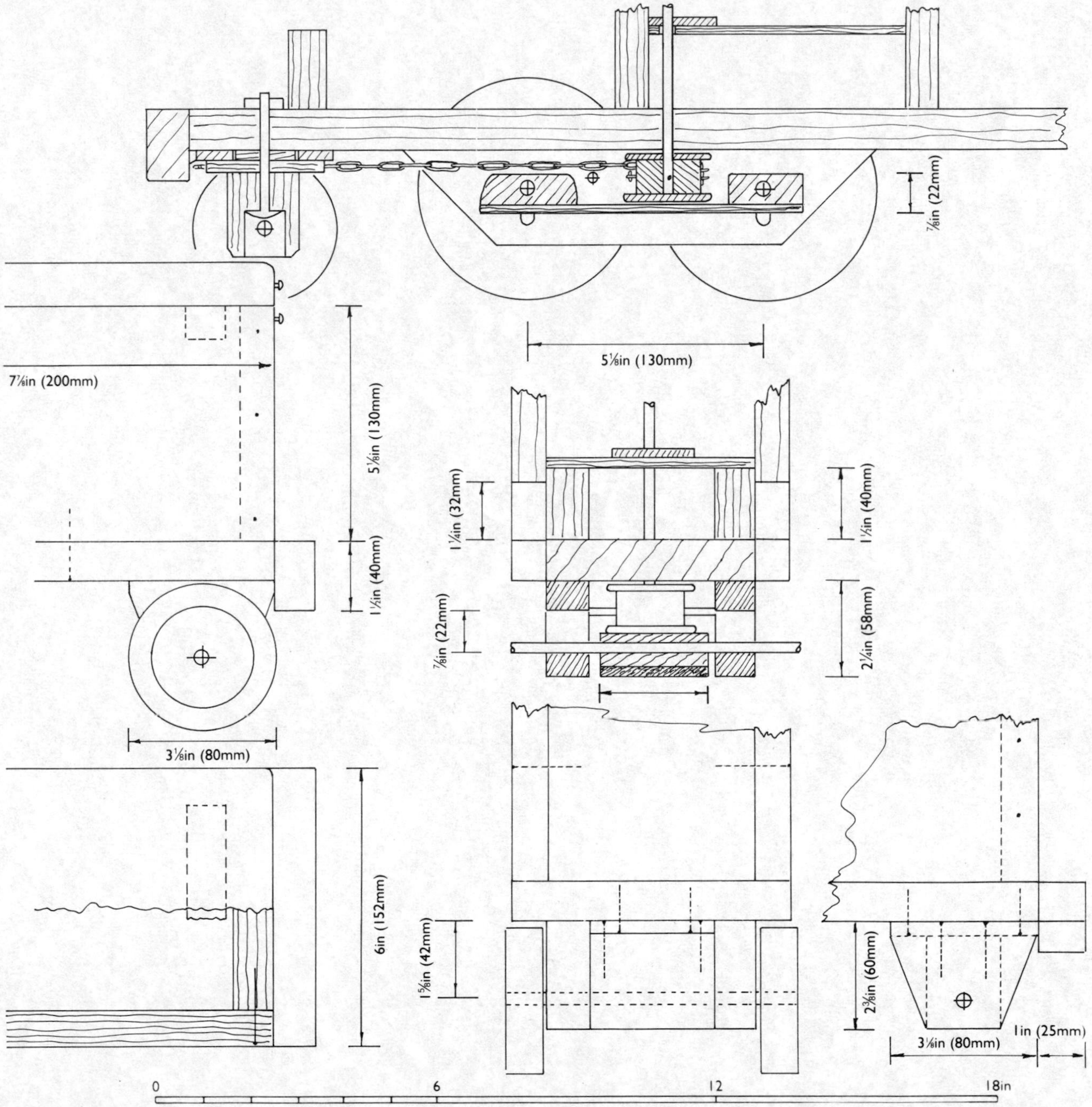
7⅞in (200mm)
5⅛in (130mm)
1½in (40mm)
3⅛in (80mm)
6in (152mm)
1⅝in (42mm)
5⅛in (130mm)
⅞in (22mm)
1¼in (32mm)
⅞in (22mm)
1½in (40mm)
2¼in (58mm)
2⅜in (60mm)
3⅛in (80mm)
1in (25mm)
0
6
12
18in

TOYS FOR THE VERY YOUNG

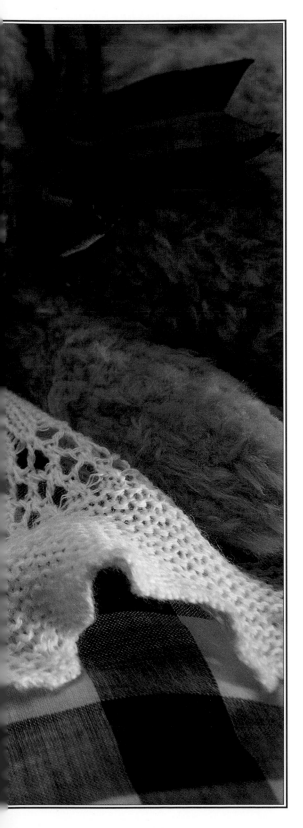

BATHTUB BOAT

This is a strong, unsinkable tug with a short, wide and solid hull. The funnel is slotted over a short stub of dowel which is set into the deck in front of the cabin. The cabin is a solid, rounded block which is glued to the deck.

This is a bathtub boat for very young children, and there are obvious benefits in keeping the design simple and uncluttered. The grooves in the deck are the only detail.

MATERIALS

1⅛in x 3⅛in (30mm x 80mm) pine
  or hardwood
¾in x 3⅛in (18mm x 80mm) pine
  or hardwood
¼in (6mm) dowel
Offcut for cabin and funnel
Epoxy resin glue

TOOLS

Jigsaw, pillar drill

1 Make a half-template of the deck plan from cardboard. Cut the hull block to shape with a jigsaw, mount the block on the carving board described on pages 78-9 and carve it to shape.

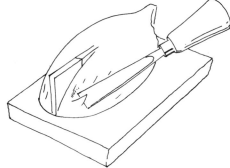

2 Remove the hull, place it, deck upwards, in the vice and saw or chisel planks longitudinally along the deck.

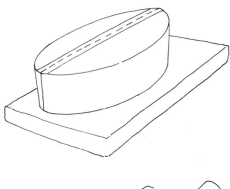

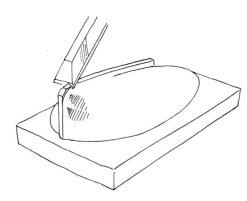

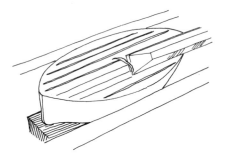

3 Lay the hull, deck downwards, on the plank for the sides, and draw round it. Use the half-template again, this time drawing on it the inside line for the sides. This is not a fixed distance from the outer edge of the hull, since the sides of the tug narrow in a 'tumblehome' at the stern, and from amidships aft the vessel's widest point is the deckline.

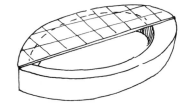

4 Take the deck plank and with a jigsaw cut out the inside line first.

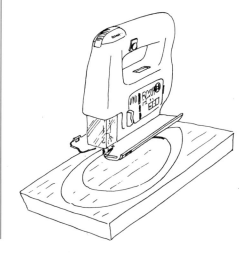

5 Smooth the sawcut with a rasp, or a piece of coarse sandpaper held against a curved block. Cut the outer line of the deck, leaving about ³⁄₁₆in (4mm) of waste all round.

6 Glue the bulwarks to the deck. When the glue is dry, trim the deck flush with the side of the hull. Then, at the stern, carve the tumblehome with a sharp chisel.
  Sandpaper the hull, rounding every corner and sharp edge.

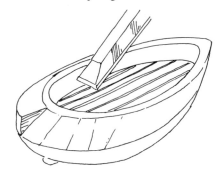

7 Shape the cabin and glue it in position on the deck. Drill the ¼in (6mm) angled hole in the deck for the funnel. Drill another hole of the same size in the bottom of the funnel and glue the funnel to the dowel.

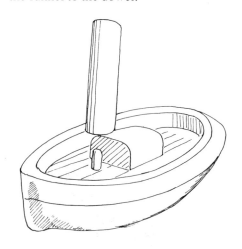

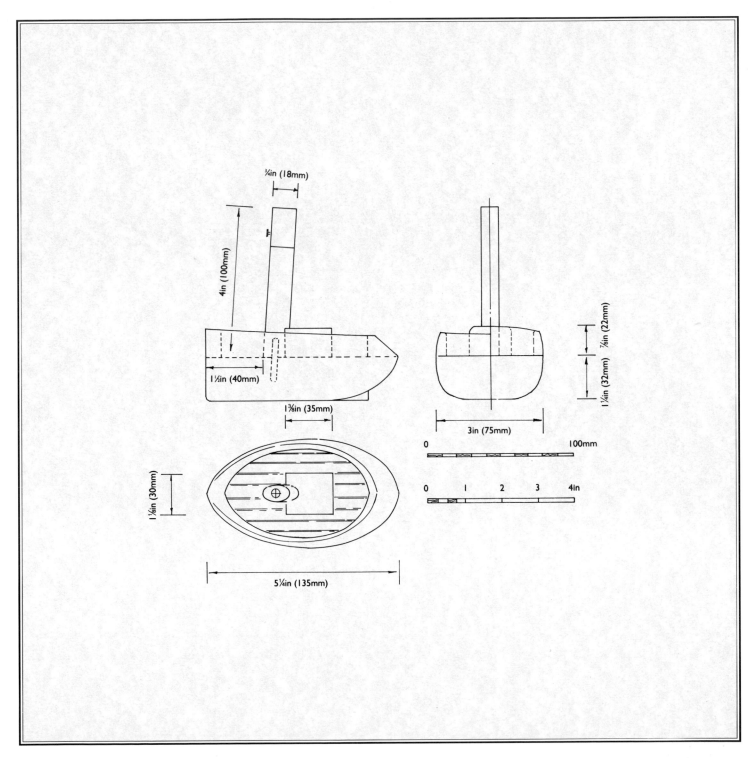

¾in (18mm)

4in (100mm)

1½in (40mm)

1⅜in (35mm)

⅞in (22mm)

1¼in (32mm)

3in (75mm)

0   100mm

0   1   2   3   4in

1⅛in (30mm)

5¼in (135mm)

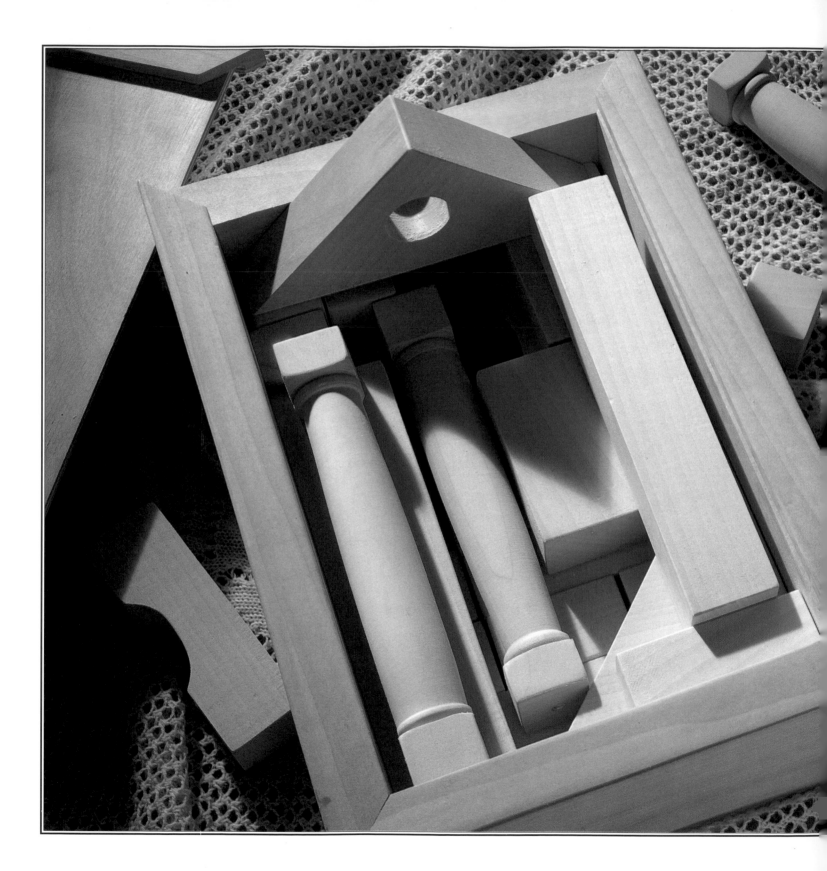

BUILDING BLOCKS

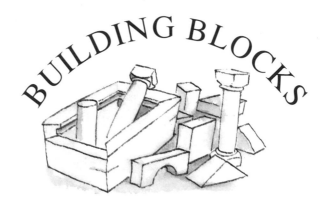

The box and building blocks illustrated are made of limewood. Heavy, silky-smooth and attractive, wood of this kind is the best choice since the aim is to stimulate your child's imagination and make handling the toy a pleasure.

An even, dense timber such as limewood is ideal for making building blocks, but if you cannot find a supplier of this or a similar wood (such as beech, cherry, sycamore or birch) use parana pine, which is available from most builder's merchants. Whichever wood you choose, make sure that it is thoroughly sanded, and does not have any cracks or splinters.

MATERIALS

BOX
¾in x 4¼in (18mm x 108mm)
  hardwood
¼in (6mm) plywood
BLOCKS
1½in x 2in (40mm x 50mm)
hardwood

TOOLS

Router with ¼in (6.3mm) straight cutter

BOX

1 The four corners of this box are mitred and then reinforced with slips inserted across the corners after the joints have been glued. Some skill is needed to plane the 45-degree mitres. Keep your block plane sharp, to prevent difficulty. The rebate in the bottom of the box, and the groove near the top, are cut with a router. The box should be made before the blocks.

2 Choose a fine strip of timber and saw it to the width shown in the plans. The sides of the strip must be parallel, otherwise the rebate and groove will not merge at the corners. Plane the strip and then rout out the rebate and the groove.

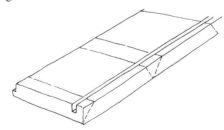

3 Mark off the sides and saw the mitres as accurately as you can. Holding the wood strip in the vice as illustrated, use a sharp cross-cut handsaw and do not press too hard.

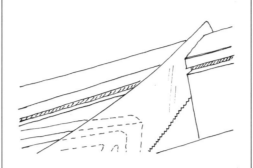

4 Plane each mitre in turn and never stray over the mitre marks. Plane all eight faces of the joint and then number them off and check that the angle made by the two sides when the mitres are pressed together is 90 degrees.

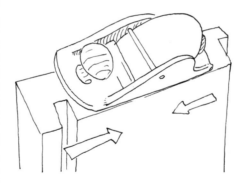

5 Lay the sides in a row, in their correct order, with their inside faces downwards. Tape the outer sides together with masking tape. Turn them onto their side and pull the two ends together to form the box. You will have to adjust one or two mitres before the box pulls together neatly, and check, while the parts are together, that the grooves and rebate meet at the corners. These, too, may have to be trimmed back with a chisel before the sides are glued together.

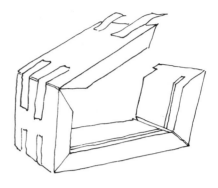

6 When you are happy with the joints, cut out a base for the box from ¼in (6mm) plywood or MDF, and trim it so that it fits into the rebate at the bottom of the box.

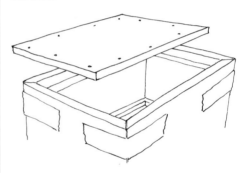

7 Now remove the base and release the last piece of tape holding the four sides together. Unfasten one of the short ends from the strip, and use the circular saw to saw from its top a strip about ½in (12mm) wide. The thin top

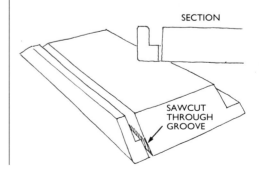

SECTION

SAWCUT THROUGH GROOVE

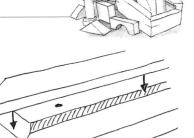

strip which you have just sawn off will be glued onto the top of the plywood lid of the box.

8 Glue the four sides of the box together, holding the corners together with masking tape. Insert the bottom of the box to hold the sides square. When the glue is dry, set the fence and a depth stop on the circular saw and saw the incisions at the corners of the box.

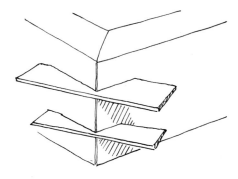

CLAMP HOLDS
STOP TO FENCE

FENCE

9 Plane a strip of suitable wood to fit into the saw groove, cut it to length and glue a strip into each groove. When the glue is dry, chisel off the waste and rub down the outside of the box with sandpaper.

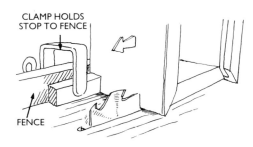

10 Cut the lid from a piece of ¼in (6mm) birch-faced plywood. Use a very sharp plane to slightly bevel its

top surface, so that it slides readily into the groove at the top of the box. Now press the lid right into the box and mark on the lid the points where the grooves on each side of the box run out into the open face of the mitre. Remove the lid, square across these marks and saw off the waste.

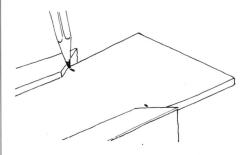

11 Take the thin top edge which was removed from the side before the box was glued together, and glue it to the edge of the lid. You can hold it in position with two short pins nailed from the underside of the lid.

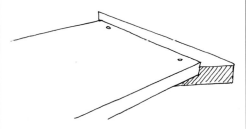

12 Now fit a thin sliver of wood into the small rebate which remains at the underside edge of the lid, glue it there and hold it with masking tape. When the glue is dry, trim the sliver flush with both the underside of the lid and the outside of the thin covering strip. Sand the outside of the box, with the lid in place.

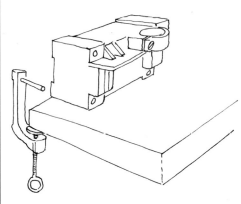

BUILDING BLOCKS

13 The blocks can be all shapes and sizes, and either square or rectangular in section. Try to include some pillars, wedges and arches as well as regular-shaped boxes. Sand them smooth with the belt sander mounted on its side.

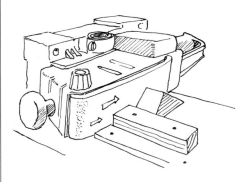

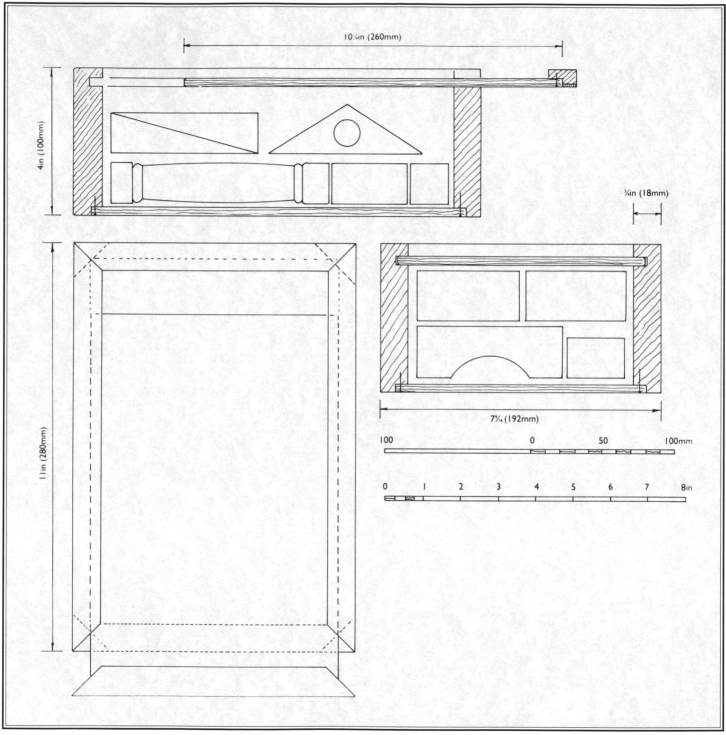

10¼in (260mm)

4in (100mm)

¼in (18mm)

11in (280mm)

7⁹⁄₁₆ (192mm)

100   0   50   100mm

0   1   2   3   4   5   6   7   8in

TOOLS
AND
SKILLS

TOOLS

SAWS

CIRCULAR SAW

The circular saw is used for making straight sawcuts. There are usually two fences available on the table. One bears against the edge of the plank, and is used for making cuts parallel to that edge. The angle fence bears against a side of the workpiece, and guides it into the blade, making a cross-grain sawcut.

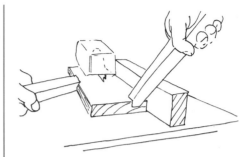

PARALLEL FENCE

ANGLE FENCE

Safety
Always work decisively and with great concentration while the saw blade is spinning. Never start the saw until the fences are adjusted, and the wood is ready for sawing. Use sticks to press the work sideways against the fence, and into the blade, as illustrated on the right. Whenever possible, use the safety guard which covers the blade. Always arrange excellent lighting when you are using the saw. A single fluorescent tube emits a flickering light which will make the rotating saw appear at times to be stationary. This stroboscopic effect is very dangerous, particularly if the saw is being used in this light for long periods. To eliminate the effect, fit a second tube, or use alternative lights when using the circular saw.

Blade types
Circular saws can be fitted with a range of blades. Multiple-toothed, tungsten-tipped blades are recommended, since they stay sharp and are quieter than high-speed steel blades. If your saw table has a rise-and-fall adjustment, set the blade so that it protrudes by no more than ¼in (6mm) above the top surface of the wood being cut. This should result in a clean, relatively chip-free sawcut.

Fences
Try to avoid using the circular saw without using the fences. These control the direction of the cut and prevent the saw from snatching or jamming. Set up the parallel fence for making parallel sawcuts, remembering to include in your calculations the width of the sawcut when you are adjusting the fence. For angled cross-cuts, use the adjustable guide. Where possible, hold the wood against the fence with one hand only, and allow the fence to control and steady the work. This will help to prevent the saw from jamming. If a number of components of the same length are to be cut using the angled guide, set up a fence as illustrated, to locate the wood

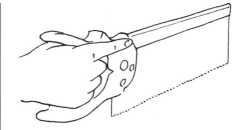

before it is sawn. If the parallel fence is used instead, the sawn-off pieces might jam or be thrown off the saw table by the revolving blade.

JIGSAW

The jigsaw makes curved sawcuts. Those fitted with an orbital cutting action cut more quickly and are easier to control. The electronic speed control is an advantage when making delicate sawcuts. The jigsaw illustrated can be fitted with a dust-extraction system, which in removing the dust leaves the operator a clear view of the cut he is making. A useful table attachment, also illustrated, can be fitted to the workbench, and used to make precise cuts in small pieces of wood.

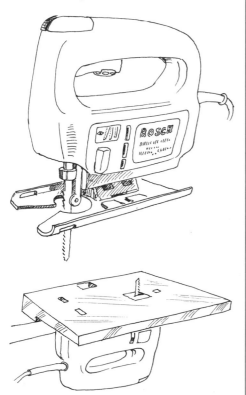

Safety
Always clamp or support your work in the vice, allowing room for the blade underneath. Keep both hands on the tool: one controls the speed of the cut, the other its direction. Never allow your hands to stray under the workpiece, and keep the electric cord well away from the blade.

Blades
A great variety of blades is available for the jigsaw illustrated. The two blades you will find the most useful are the T101D for cutting straight lines and curves in wood up to about 2⅜in (60mm) thick, and the fine-toothed T119BO for cutting intricate shapes in wood up to ⅝in (15mm) thick.

TENON SAW

If you do not already possess a tenon saw, choose a small one, with a brass rather than a steel stiffening bar along the top of the blade. Hold the saw as illustrated, with the first finger resting

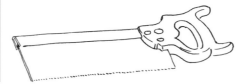

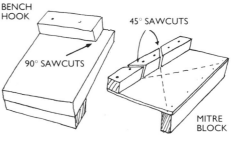

BENCH HOOK

90° SAWCUTS

45° SAWCUTS

MITRE BLOCK

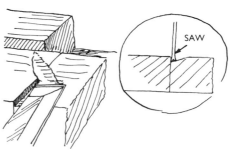

SAW

against the side of the handle. Use the tenon saw in conjunction with the bench hook and mitre block, illustrated, which are easily made in the workshop. For making a clean and accurate across-the-grain sawcut, incise the cutting line with a knife, chisel away a thin slice of wood on the waste side of the line and start the saw off in the resulting groove.

FRETSAW

The fretsaw is a lightweight, delicate tool with a fine blade, which can cut intricate shapes in thin wood or similar materials. Blades are bought in a pack which contains a variety of thicknesses and tooth sizes. For most of the projects

described in this book, size W1/0 32 will be satisfactory. The saw cuts on its down stroke, so fit the blade with the teeth pointing downwards. The teeth on the finest blades are so fine that the only way to tell which way to fit them is to run your finger up and down the teeth.

Fit the blade in the bottom clamp nearest the handle. You might find it necessary to tighten the wingnut with pliers or a small screwdriver. Loosen the top tensioning wingnut and, pressing the frame of the saw against the bench, feed the top of the blade into the top clamp and tighten. If the blade seems a little slack, tension it with the top wingnut. The blade should be tight, and ring when plucked.

SAW TABLE

The saw is held by the handle, with the frame tucked under the arm. It requires a gentle vertical motion from the arm to make it cut. About 2in (50mm) of movement is all that is needed; any more might stress the blade and break it. With the saw held in this confined position under the arm, it is impossible to steer the saw. So the saw must be fed and steered into the blade by the left hand. To make this easier, nail together the simple saw table illustrated.

This is held in the vice, and projects below the bench.

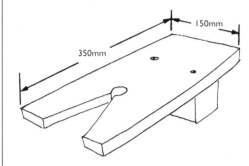

150mm

350mm

Hold the work at the apex of the 'V' and keep the saw blade moving inside the circle. If you practise on some waste wood, feeding the wood slowly and keeping the saw blade moving (even when turning a sharp corner or withdrawing the blade) you will quickly find this a versatile tool for fine detailing work.

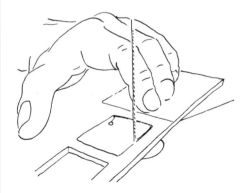

COPING SAW

This has coarser teeth than the fretsaw. The blade is held in tension by the

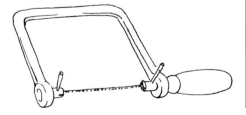

spring steel saw frame. The angle of the blade is adjusted by the swivels at each end of the blade. The coping saw is held with both hands, with the blade usually oriented so that it cuts on the push stroke.

Most tool stores offer a saw-sharpening service, which you should use when your saw becomes difficult to control or push. When you are proficient with the tenon saw or the handsaw, you can ask the store to reduce the offset of the teeth. Known as the 'set', this arrangement of the teeth clears dust from the sawcut, so that the teeth do not become clogged up. When you can saw a clean, straight line with confidence, giving the saw a reduced set will accelerate the speed at which the teeth cut through the wood.

PLANES

The two planes needed for making the toys described in this book are illustrated below. The smoothing plane is the larger of the two, and is useful for general work. The shoulder or block plane, which is fitted with a low-angle blade, is used for delicate work, particularly cross-grain and end-grain planing.

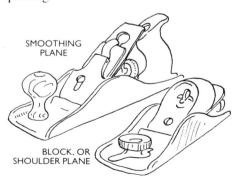

SMOOTHING PLANE

BLOCK, OR SHOULDER PLANE

USING A PLANE

Hold the plane with both hands. The left hand holds the knob at the front of the plane, and applies a slight downwards pressure, while the right hand propels the plane forwards. If you practise this deliberate action, particularly as the plane enters and leaves the cut, you will be able plane a straight edge.

Planing end grain

Planing end grain can be hard work. Lubricate the sole of the plane with a rub or two of candle wax, and take one of the following precautions to prevent the wood splintering:

Plane the end-grain surface before trimming the sides. This way you can cut off the splintered wood after the end grain has been planed.

Plane from both ends towards the middle. (This is not recommended for accurate work.)

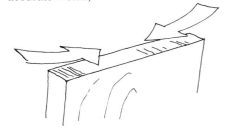

Arrange a sacrificial block of similar wood, to press against the end of the piece being trimmed. It can split and then be discarded.

When planing mitres, use the plane in a diagonal direction, as illustrated.

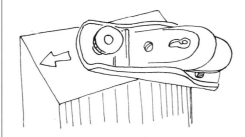

Planing an edge square

To learn how to plane an edge square, first practise moving the plane from side to side as you push it forward. The cutting profile of the plane is such that the blade will cut slightly more wood at its centre than at the sides. By trailing a finger from each hand you can steer the tool so as to take advantage of this unequal cut. Provided the sole of the plane is pressed flat against the workpiece, and you plane before each cut the line the blade should take, you will soon be able to square up a piece of wood.

CHISELS

You will need three chisels for making these projects. All bevel-edged, they are ⅝in (15mm), ⅜in (9mm) and ¼in (6mm) wide. Bevel-edged chisels are not tough tools. They should always be kept sharp, and handled with delicacy. Hold the chisel as illustrated, and use both hands to control it. Rather than push the chisel with your arms, apply your body weight to press the chisel into the wood. If you keep your elbows and arms close to your body while using the chisel, this action will almost be automatic.

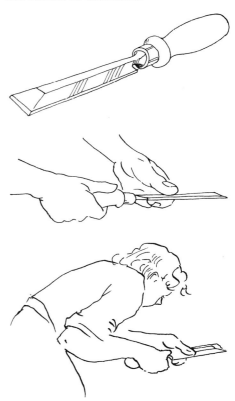

Safety

Chisels are easier and safer to use if they are extremely sharp. Instructions for sharpening edged tools are given on

pages 130-1. Remember to always keep all your body (including your fingers!) behind the edge of the chisel, and ensure that the workpiece is fixed firmly before starting work.

GOUGES

These are held and used in the same way as chisels. Gouges are substantial tools

and can be used with a mallet. If you do not have a woodcarving mallet, find a

short length of 2in (50mm) diameter branch that has been cut for firewood, and use that instead. Square carpenter's mallets are heavy and cumbersome. As with a chisel, you should almost always aim to remove a shaving with each pass of the gouge. When you first use the gouge, practise the slight scooping motion that lifts the cutting edge out of the wood.

SKILLS

SHARPENING

The instructions here are for sharpening edged tools such as knives, chisels, plane blades and gouges.

First you must recognize when your tools are blunt. Sometimes this will be obvious: the tool may have a gashed edge, highlighted if you hold the tip towards a strong light source, or the cutter may leave scratch marks as it slices through the wood. If you are careful in picking your tools up and placing them back on the bench these gross faults will be quite uncommon. It is more likely that you will simply find a

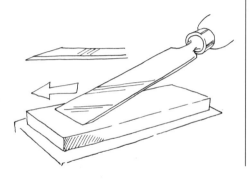

job harder work than you anticipated. If so, you must check the blade. If you are using a chisel, try to slice off the corner of an offcut with a vertical chop. It should be easy. If it is not, sharpen the blade. If you are using a penknife or a plane, hold a piece of paper against the edge of the blade, and slice slowly into the paper. If the knife cleaves through it cleanly the blade is sharp. If the paper tears, or the knife hesitates, the blade is blunt.

You will need a medium and a fine oilstone, and a leather strop. For sharpening gouges, you will also need a curved slip stone.

The sharpening procedure is as follows. Lubricate the medium oilstone. Hold the blade as illustrated, with its sharpening bevel flat against the oilstone, and grind it along the stone, keeping the blade at a constant angle. Repeat this five times, or until you raise a slight roughness at the tip of the blade.

Turn the blade over, hold it flat against the stone and push it forwards.

This will grind off the burr. Do this once, then repeat the first stage, keeping the tool at the same angle as before, but pressing more gently. Remove the burr, and repeat the first stage once more.

Now lubricate the fine oilstone, and repeat the whole process a few more times.

Finish by using the strop. You can buy stropping compound from men's hairdressers, and there are normally two grades of compound in the pack. Rub the compounds onto two strips of leather. Then, repeating the process described above, drag the sharpening bevel five times down the strop, then once more with the blade flat against the leather to remove the burr.

Repeat the process on the finest compound. If you look closely at the mark left by the blade on the strop you will be able to tell whether you have obtained a good edge. If the blade leaves a row of fine parallel lines you will have to return to using the fine oilstone to remove the minute nicks that have

remained in the blade.

Once you have obtained a good edge, do your best to preserve it. Take care picking up and putting down your tools. Never, for example, place a plane flat on the workbench. Make sure that you strop your tools regularly.

GOUGES
Gouges are sharpened as described above, except that you should apply a rolling action to the tool as you grind the outside bevel. If you grind the outside bevel on the flat surface of the slip stone, you will slowly form a groove. Use the same groove every time; as it deepens, more of the curved edge will be ground at each pass of the gouge.

Remove the burr every five strokes with a slipstone.

Make the stropping board shown below. Rub compound into the grooves

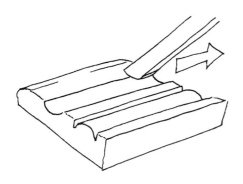

made by the tools and use the board as a finishing strop.

USING A HAMMER

Before driving in a nail, clean the face of the hammer with some scrap sandpaper, since you will be more likely to bend the nail if the face of the hammer is dirty. When you plan to hammer in a nail longer than 1½in (40mm), drill a pilot hole to prevent it splitting the wood. Also drill a pilot hole if you are going to nail close to the end of a board or if the grain of the wood is weak and short.

If you find it difficult to keep the nail in position before hitting it, hold it with long-nosed pliers, and release it after a few blows. If you cannot hammer in a nail without bending it, check that it is not hitting something in the wood, such as another nail. If this is not causing the nail to bend, and you have drilled a pilot hole for one of the reasons given above, check that the pilot hole is nearly as deep as the nail is long and of a slightly smaller diameter.

If you still have a problem, make sure that you are using the right hammer. Use a small pin hammer for gimp pins, veneer pins and panel pins, and a larger hammer for bigger nails. If the hammer is too heavy it will drive in the nail too fast, probably bending it, while if it is too light it will bounce off the nail. If you are still having difficulty despite using the correct size of hammer, change the way you hold it. The hammer should be used in a radial manner, pivotting at the wrist. The handle is kept level with the top of the nail, so that it is lowered as the nail is driven in. Press your

forefinger along the handle to provide greater control of the hammer.

USING A MARKING GAUGE

To use a marking gauge, tilt it slightly so that the scriber trails behind the stock, and make sure that the fence is pressed tightly against the timber you want to mark. The marking gauge is normally held with one hand, but if at first you find this difficult, hold the wood in the vice and use both hands to control the gauge.

ROUTING

The router illustrated over the page is a versatile and powerful tool. It has a plunge mechanism, and can take a variety of ¼in (6.3mm) shank cutters. The cutters you will need to make the toys in this book are also illustrated. Tungsten-carbide cutters are more expensive than the high-speed steel variety, but they retain their cutting edge for much longer, and are worth the extra cost.

Safety
Wear goggles and ear muffs when using a router, and make sure that the lighting is excellent. Keep a vacuum cleaner to hand, to remove dust.

USING A ROUTER
The router can be used in a number of slightly different ways.

Copy routing
Disconnect the power supply and fit the ⅛in (3.2mm) cutter in the router and

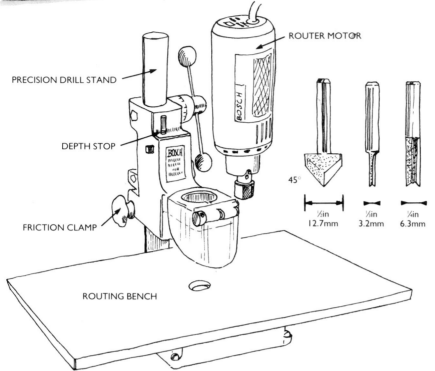

PRECISION DRILL STAND

DEPTH STOP

FRICTION CLAMP

ROUTER MOTOR

45°

½in
12.7mm

⅛in
3.2mm

¼in
6.3mm

ROUTING BENCH

hands to venture close to the revolving cutter.

Reconnect the power supply to the router. Fit the blank into or onto the template, then place the template over the template pin and hold it there with your left hand. Start the router. Lower the router, and plunge the cutter into the blank. If the friction knob is adjusted correctly, the router will stay in place while you tighten the knob sufficiently to prevent the router from lifting out of the blank.

Now, using both hands, move the template board so that it butts up against the pin, as illustrated below. The router will then make a precise copy of the template. When the router has released the waste wood from the centre of the blank, raise the cutter.

tighten it. Clamp the plywood plate which retains the template guide pin onto the routing bench.

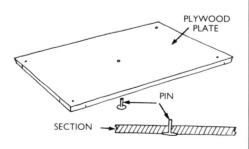

PLYWOOD PLATE

PIN

SECTION

Position the pin so that the router bit is directly above it. Set the depth stop to prevent the router from plunging onto the template guide.

Make up one of the template boards illustrated on the right. The larger boards are tacked to the workpiece with pins.

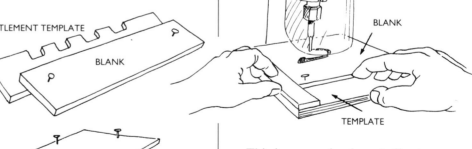

BATTLEMENT TEMPLATE

BLANK

Small objects should be held between blocks tacked to the template, and either nailed or taped down to the template. Under no circumstances allow your

BLANK

TEMPLATE

This is a very simple and effective system, and shapes can be copy-routed

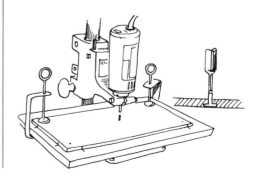

from ¼in (6mm) stock in a single pass of the cutter blade, as illustrated.

Ensure that you are using a sharp cutter, and do not let the motor revolutions drop below 70 percent of their normal running speed.

A complex template presents a different problem. If the template is a complex shape, simplify the task by rounding the corners of the template to allow the pin easier movement, and practise moving the template around the pin before fitting the blank and cutting your first shape.

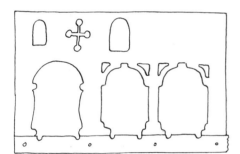

Most of the forces applied to the template board are borne by the template guide pin. You must make certain that the templates are not so delicate that they bend when the board is pulled hard against the pin.

MITRE CUTTING

Set the mitre cutter and fence as illustrated.

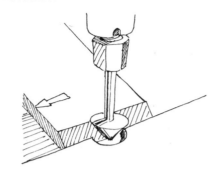

Make sure that the fence is tacked down to the mitre table before testing the set-up on some scrap board. Feed the board against the direction of the cutter. Make

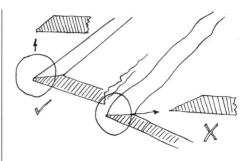

sure that your hands remain well clear of the router bit.

This is a very simple procedure, but it is impossible to do it successfully if the mitre cutter removes the fine edge of the board being mitred. Make sure when setting up the equipment that the end cut of the board is not eroded by the cutter. It is better to stop the mitre slightly short of the very point of the edge rather than risk a wobbly and irregular mitre joint, as illustrated above.

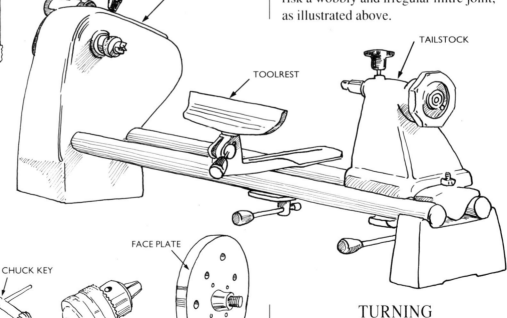

HEADSTOCK

TOOLREST

TAILSTOCK

FACE PLATE

CHUCK KEY

HEADSTOCK OR TAILSTOCK CHUCK

TAILSTOCK TAPER

TURNING

The illustration above shows a good-quality lathe and some of the accessories that can be bought for it. The spindle in

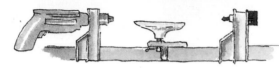

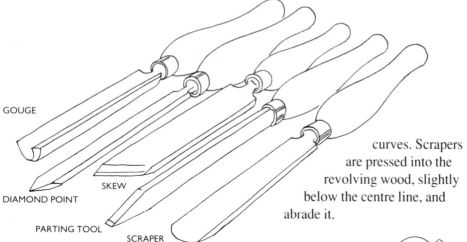

GOUGE

DIAMOND POINT

SKEW

PARTING TOOL

SCRAPER

the headstock end rotates the workpiece, and held by the centre point of the tailstock. The tool rest is adjustable for height and angle.

The face plate is an alternative headstock fitting to the chiselpointed live centre. This screws into the headstock bearing, and work which is screwed to the face plate can be turned, in many cases without the need of the tailstock centre.

The tools shown above are very strong, with thick steel blades to dissipate the heat generated in the turning, and long handles for a good grip. The range illustrated below will be sufficient for most turning needs. The skew chisels and parting tool are sharpened with a bevel on both sides, and cut with a slicing or planing action. These are sharpened on an oilstone in the same way as a chisel or plane blade.

Gouges and scrapers are ground to a steep, ragged edge on a grindstone, and are much more aggressive cutters. The gouges are used for reducing stock quickly to size and for cutting delicate

curves. Scrapers are pressed into the revolving wood, slightly below the centre line, and abrade it.

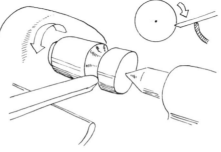

The diamond-point scraper, which is also rough-sharpened on the grindstone, is a versatile tool. It can be used for reducing square-sectioned stock to a cylinder, and for delicate shaping.

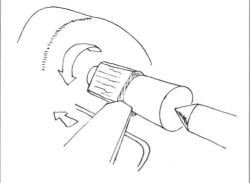

The parting tool is used for cutting or parting the turning from the waste wood once the shaping is completed.

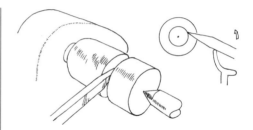

When you are using a lathe, ensure that you have excellent lighting. Wear safety glasses, and never move quickly. Work should be deliberate and careful. It is very easy to ruin a piece of turning with a careless movement, and unless you remember the dangers of the machine you are using you can easily injure your hands as well.

The following sections give brief instructions on using the lathe to make the components described in the book. It is not meant to be an instruction manual for a wood-turner.

TURNING WHEELS

The wheels for the toys are turned on the face plate. They are held in place by a captured bolt mounted on the face plate. Take a ¼in (6mm) coach or engineering bolt, and drill a small conical recess in its threaded end, using a metalworking drill.

Cut a disc of ½in (12mm) scrap plywood to fit onto the face plate, and screw it in position, screwing into the disc from the back face of the face plate. Use four screws to hold it in place, and scribe a location mark on the top of the disc and on the adjacent rim of the face plate. Now fit a ¼in (6mm) metalworking drill in the tailstock chuck, start the lathe and bore a hole in

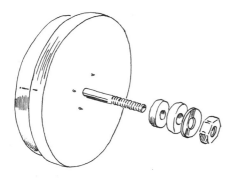

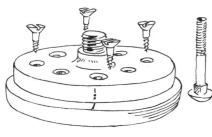

the centre of the wooden disc. Stop the lathe, unscrew the disc and carve a recess in the back of the disc for the head of the bolt. Poke the bolt into the hole and check that, with the bolt in position, the disc lies flat against the

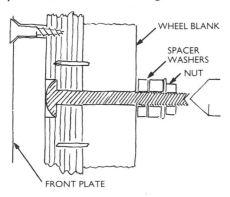

WHEEL BLANK

SPACER WASHERS

NUT

FRONT PLATE

face plate. Screw the disc back onto the front of the face plate, using the same screws in the same screw holes.

Tap a few panel pins into the face plate immediately surrounding the bolt, to help anchor the wheel while it is being turned.

Make up a few washers and wooden tubes of different lengths to press against the wheel, and the assembly is ready for use.

The instructions here refer to a single wheel. It is, of course, not possible to make four wheels in one operation, but quicker to turn four as a group.

First drill the ¼in (6mm) centre hole for the wheel, and then cut round the perimeter with a jigsaw. Plane the back face of the wheel until it is smooth.

Slip the wheel along the bolt, fit one or two wooden washers against the hub of the wheel, and then fit the nut on the bolt. Turn the face plate by hand, holding the nut in a spanner to tighten the wheel against the face plate.

Slide the tailstock centre into the conical recess in the bolt end, and lubricate the point with a drop of oil.

Switch on the lathe, and use the diamond-point cutter as in the illustrated sequence to cut the outside shape of the

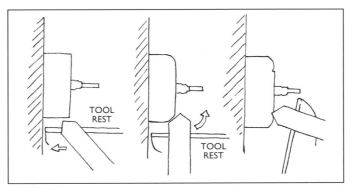

TOOL REST

TOOL REST

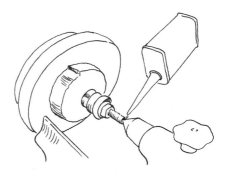

tyre, right round to the wheel hub.

Change tools and, with the small, half-round scraper, cut out the hub.

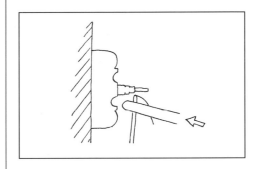

Remove the tools, slide the tool rest away from the workpiece, and sand the wheel, holding coarse sandpaper against a polyethylene-foam block. Switch the lathe off and let the sandpaper slow the rotating wheel down.

Repeat the whole procedure for the other wheels.

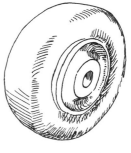

TURNING PULLEYS AND RATCHETS

These are turned in the same way as the wheel. Where it is only the very edge of a thin piece of MDF or plywood that is being turned, it is a good idea to slip a small-diameter wooden washer behind the workpiece, to move it out a little from the face plate. If the nut is tightened sufficiently there will be plenty of friction between the washers to prevent the disc from slipping as it is turned.

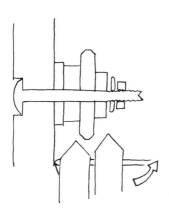

Use the diamond point to cut the radiused edge of the ratchet, and a very small-diameter home-made curved scraper to make the groove in the pulley, once the diamond point has trimmed its perimeter.

When the perimeter of the ratchet is finished, release it from the lathe and, holding it onto a piece of scrap wood, chop out the ratchet. Each nick in the wheel is shaped by four cuts, each one slightly encroaching on the previous, as illustrated. Cut the ratchet free hand, since it does not matter if it is slightly irregular.

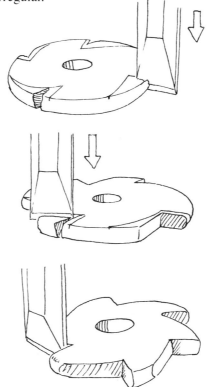

TURNING LARGE BEARING RINGS

Place both ring blanks on the face plate centre bolt and clamp them together with the washers and nut. Fit the centre point of the tailstock into the end cone of the bolt, and lubricate it.

Now use the diamond-point scraper to trim the outer perimeter of the two discs. When this is done, sand the outer edge.

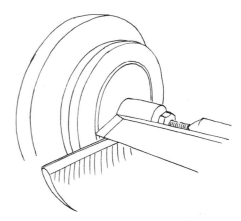

To extract the centre small-diameter disc from the upper disc in the bearing, hold the small skew chisel as illustrated, and press it into the point where you want to make the cut. The skew chisel will make a clean, sharp-edged incision, and the outer perimeter ring will fall free and be caught by the face plate bolt in the centre

If you are making the steam crane, you should drill the holes for the stub dowels in the perimeters of the two discs before removing the centre section.

CYLINDERS AND PILLARS

These are turned between centres on the lathe. The live centre grips and turns the wood, and the tailstock centre holds the end steady. Cylinders are turned into towers and pillars, so when your turning has achieved what you want, you can dispense with the remainder of the instructions, sand the work with a strip of sandpaper backed by masking tape, and remove it from the centres with the parting tool.

Take the square-sectioned blank for the pillar. Find the centre at each end, and mark the centres with a tap of the centre punch.

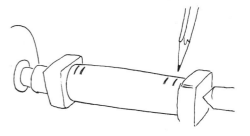

Place the blank in the vice and roughly trim away the corners with a chisel.

Place the blank in the lathe, and set the tool rest parallel to the workpiece and level with its centre line.

Use the diamond-point tool, working towards the headstock to reduce the blank to a rough cylinder.

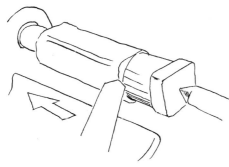

When you think you have achieved this, lightly touch the side of the revolving cylinder farthest from you – if your fingers are knocked back by the workpiece, it needs more trimming.

When you have trimmed the blank to a rough cylinder, switch off the lathe and raise the tool rest. The top of the rest should be level with the top of the cylinder.

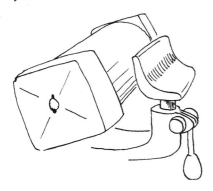

Use the large skew chisel, holding it as illustrated, flat against the centre of the cylinder, with its cutting edge just clear of the wood.

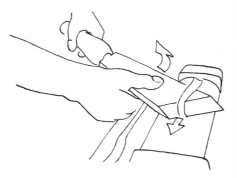

This is how you introduce the tool into its cut. By just twisting it slightly, it will begin to slice away the roughness on the top of the cylinder. Practise holding and twisting the chisel, and then start the lathe.

Lay the chisel on the wood and, holding it steady with both hands, twist it slightly, just a fraction, enough to remove the thinnest of shavings. Keep your hands and arms locked in position, and move the skew chisel along the tool rest. Do not force the chisel along. No purpose is served by pressing hard against the tool rest: it is merely a pivot point, and to press hard will make it difficult to move the chisel.

When you have finished the stroke in one direction, lift off the chisel and, starting again in the centre, work in the opposite direction.

Switch off the lathe. Your cylinder should look smooth and fairly regular. If there are little bumps and undulations in the middle they have probably been caused by a knot, or by gripping and pressing the tool too hard, causing the wood to 'whip'.

Use a pencil to mark on the cylinder the position for the beads.

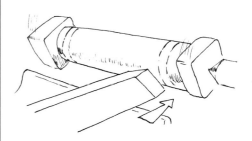

Lower the tool rest.
Use the point of an inverted skew chisel to incise the marks for the bead.

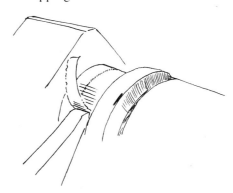

Use the parting tool to remove the narrow band of waste above the bead. Repeat at the opposite end of the pillar. The parting tool is used to cut a tangential cut, as illustrated. To increase the depth of the cut, the handle of the tool is raised slightly. Increase the width of the cut by making a second, overlapping cut to the first.

Stop the lathe and raise the tool rest. Using the skew chisel on its side, reduce

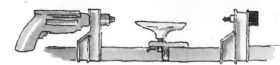

the diameter of the pillar, taking more wood from the ends by the beads than from the centre.

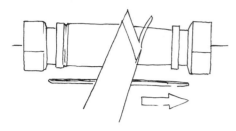

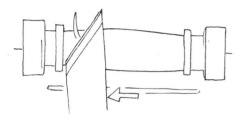

Sand the pillar and, if you feel confident, use the very bottom point of the sharp edge of the skew chisel to snip a narrow bevel on the hard top edges of

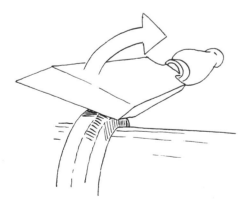

the beads. When the bead is sanded, the sandpaper will round off the bead.

Cut the pillar to length with the parting tool. Saw off the remaining stubs in the ends after removing the pillar from the lathe.

TURNING TURRETS FOR THE BATTLESHIP

Turn a cylinder of wood (see above). Before using the chisel, fit a ¼in (6.3mm) drill bit into the tailstock chuck, and drill a hole up the centre of the turret, penetrating no more than ½in (12mm).

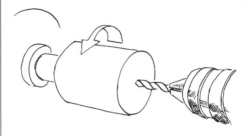

Provided the drill exerts a gentle pressure on the block, it will remain pinioned on the live centre.

Now replace the drill chuck with the centrepoint, and clamp it into the hole in the base of the turret.

Use the parting tool to make an incision at the top of the turret. While you are using the parting tool, square up the bottom of the turret as well.

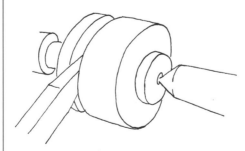

When this is done, stop the lathe and raise the tool rest. The remaining work is carried out with the skew chisel. First cut the sweep from the base of the turret to the top.

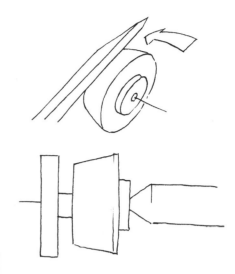

Then cut a new line, tilting the skew chisel sharply sideways down the top of the turret, until it parts the turret from the block of wood.

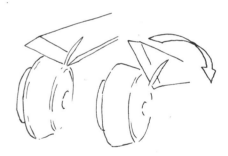

Smaller turrets are turned in the same way, except that, instead of making a hard turn at the top of the turret, you can shape it with a curve.

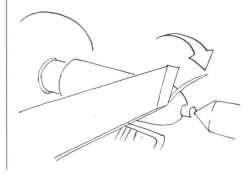

PAINTING AND VARNISHING

The little models you have made are meant to be played with. In most cases, they are not in scale, and they are far from perfect representations of the objects they imitate. It does not matter what colour they are as long as they look attractive. Nor does it matter if the paint or varnish finish is blemished.

There is just as much charm in a rough-hewn toy as in a perfectly made one. Enjoy the painting, have fun with the colours, and perhaps personalize some of the vehicles with special number plates or company names. Make each toy special, but do not worry if it is not perfect.

It is important, however, to use paints that are safe for children to play with. All the model-making paints in the Humbrol range have been tested and are safe, and Trimite sell a range of safe toy paints. Paints sold in the United Kingdom for interior domestic use are also safe, but their colours are rather subdued for toys. Because they are free from pigmentation, most varnishes and polishes do not present any health hazard. Interior clear wood finishes are also suitable.

PAINTING

Paint or varnish your toy in a dry, dust-free room. Work in steps, bringing all the components of the toy to the same stage in the finishing process before moving on to the next stage. In this way it is possible to clear up the dust caused by sanding before the painting starts, all the sealing and all the undercoating can be completed in two sessions, and only the different-coloured top coat need be applied on a piece-by-piece basis.

PAINTING THE BARN, CASTLE AND DOLL'S HOUSE

These can be painted with normal house paints, or with artist's acrylic paints. As long as the buildings look attractive, light and believable, they will be fine. The exterior of the Georgian doll's house, for example, needs only to be painted with a stone or magnolia emulsion to look right. It is not necessary to scratch in bricks and stones. The same applies to the castle. The barn, which is made from MDF, has scratched boards on it, which break up the surface, making further artistic work unnecessary.

SANDING

Dismantle the toy and sand each piece. Use 220 open cut paper, supported by a small block of stiff foam, to smooth the rough areas and remove the sharp edges. Polyethylene foam is an ideal material for the block. Small pieces can be cut from the rigid foam tubes used for lagging waterpipes.

UNDERCOATING

Use a fairly thick ('high-build') undercoat. Stir the paint well before use, and apply it thickly, running it into areas of open grain. Leave the toy to dry, sandpaper the rough areas smooth, and apply a second coat of paint to those areas that are still rough.

Wait until the paint is thoroughly dry before sanding it smooth.

TOP COATING

Use a good-quality brush for the top coat. Stir the paint thoroughly, and use a well-loaded brush, held at 45 degrees to the surface. Apply the paint slowly. The brush is working well if the paint can be seen flowing off the brush onto the undercoat. If patches of undercoat are left after the brush has passed, you have either moved the brush too quickly or you have not loaded it sufficiently. Try to avoid overbrushing. Excessive reworking of the surface will spoil the finish. If you have to touch in an area of unsatisfactory paintwork, do it as soon as you see it is necessary.

Leave the top coat to dry. Thick enamel paint will take about two days to reach satisfactory hardness.

If a second coat is required, leave the finish for two or three days, then sand and dust off the first coat before applying the second top coat.

PAINTING PROBLEMS

Areas where the paint has crept away from the undercoat are usually the result of grease on the undercoat, probably caused by excessive handling during sanding. Try to avoid handling the toy between coats. Wait until the existing paint is completely dry before sanding down the affected area, then touching in with a small brush.

SPECKLED, ROUGH FINISH

This may be caused by dust that has either fallen onto the wet paint or has been applied by the brush. Make sure you use a separate brush for dusting off the toy before painting it, and when you

are dusting it off, dust it thoroughly, otherwise the new paint brush will pick up small amounts of dust from the toy and spread it over the top coat.

A speckled finish may also be the result of poor preparation. With the exception of a high-build undercoat, which has a lot of pigmented filler incorporated in it, most of the paint finishes applied by brush leave a very fine layer, which will reveal the underlying surface blemishes. The apparent thickness of the paint as it flows from the brush is deceptive, for much of what you see going on to the wood will evaporate. It is therefore important to ensure that the undercoat is as smooth as you can make it.

A speckled finish is also caused by a reaction between the paint and the substrate. In some forms of MDF the binder which holds the material together, and gives it its smooth even finish, can be etched away by the solvents in the paint, causing the fibres of the MDF to lift. This can be over-come by applying several undercoats, and sanding down the surface after the second and third coats. Alternatively, you can seal the MDF with a coat of sealer that etches neither the existing paintwork nor the MDF binder.

An alcohol-based shellac sealer will do this. Sand down the existing paintwork thoroughly before applying the sealer with a soft paint brush. Clean the brush in methylated spirits, and leave the sealer to harden for about 30 minutes before lightly sanding it. Continue with a top coat or second undercoat, depending on the quality of the surface.

RUNS AND DRIPS

The paints recommended above are fairly fast-drying, and their outer surface glazes over within about fifteen minutes of the paint being applied. Even after this time, thickly applied paint will sag and run. Try to arrange that the surface you are painting is horizontal, and avoid applying too heavy a load of paint in one coat. Once you have applied a coat, and left it for a short while, reposition the toy, if necessary supporting the freshly painted surface on the points of drawing pins. This will enable you to paint the opposite surface.

WRINKLING AND BRUISING

If the paint finish is handled too soon after the paint has been applied, the surface skin will wrinkle and bruise. The oil-based paints described above dry from the outside inwards. A toy that is apparently dry can still have a vulnerable paint finish. The best way to ensure that the paint is thoroughly dry before adding decorative paintwork or fitting the wheels (both processes that involve handling) is to leave the toy for a few days. Two days in a warm room should be enough to dry all but the largest drips.

PAINTED DECORATIONS

Use the same oil-based paints as described above, and paint the decorations on the toy with a pointed sable or similar paint brush. A good-quality student watercolour brush is ideal. Paint all the embellishments free hand, with the minimum use of pencil or ballpoint lines and rulers as guides. Hold the brush with two hands, resting them

against a block or board, if necessary, to steady them. If you are painting intricate work on the side of, for example, the steam train, arrange a stable armrest to support your arm's weight, and allow it to move easily in the direction you will be painting.

Apply one colour at a time, and wait until the paint has begun to harden before applying a second colour. It is quite difficult to know how much decoration to put on. Plan your ideas in advance, but be prepared to stop if your toy looks finished. It is easy to overdo the decorations, and this will result in a toy that looks a little unsure of itself.

VARNISHING

The remarks above relating to the preparation and application of paint finishes also apply to varnish except that, whatever wood or MDF material you are varnishing, it is worthwhile applying a clear sealer coat and sanding it before applying the varnish.

The problem with varnish is that it reveals, even spotlights, all your mistakes during cutting, smoothing and joining. It will reveal mistakes you did

not even know you had made. In particular it will show all the smears of PVA glue that were not cleaned away quickly enough, and even coloured filler will become an embarrassing feature. The best thing to do is to try to hide these marks with paint. You will need watercolour paints, a small pointed watercolour brush and a lump of soap.

Your first sealer or varnish coat will reveal the extent of your problems. Wait until it is dry and then, using an almost dry paint brush, spot an appropriate coloured paint over the discoloured area. The purpose of spotting is to try to reproduce the tonal variations in the surface of the timber, for the tone is never uniform. The size and direction of the small marks which you paint on should be related to the general appearance of the wood's surface. Do not concentrate excessively on causing the marks to disappear. You will find that on close scrutiny everything is blemished, and you will only need to bring the worst marks to the average. Some lacquers and varnishes are rather waxy, and if you encounter problems in painting onto the surface of the varnish, rub the brush into the bar of soap before picking up the paint on the brush.

It is not so easy to disguise a dark mark in the wood. The varnish itself will usually darken the tone of the timber, and this is why the marks left by the glue and the filler are revealed. If an inappropriate black filler has been used, it can be painted out with two applications of paint. The first will be a mixture of raw sienna watercolour mixed with opaque white body-colour, and the second coat, which is applied as soon as the first is dry, will be a delicate spotted coat of burnt sienna.

When you have done your best to conceal these marks, varnish them at once, and do not sand these areas until you have applied the penultimate coat.

SUPPLIERS

Most of the materials and tools required to make the toys described in this book can be obtained from your local hardware store and hobby shop. The following list is included to help those who have difficulty in obtaining them.

DOLL'S HOUSE SUPPLIES
The Dolls House
29 The Market
Covent Garden
London WC2 8RE

MODELLING TIMBER AND TOOLS
Borcraft Miniatures
8 Fairfax View
Scotland Lane
Horsforth
Leeds
West Yorkshire LS18 5SZ

W Hobby Ltd
Knights Hill Square
London SE27 0HH

Blackwells of Hawkwell
733 London Road
Westcliff-on-Sea
Essex SS0 9ST

FINISHING MATERIALS
Fiddes and Son, Ltd
Florence Works
Brindley Road
Cardiff CF1 7IX

EPOXY RESIN GLUE
SP Systems Ltd
Cowes
Isle of Wight PO31 7EU

TOOLS
Robert Bosch Ltd
Power Tools Division
PO Box 98
Broadwater Park
North Orbital Road
Denham
Uxbridge
Middlesex UB9 5HJ

ELECTRIC-DRILL-POWERED LATHE
Wolfcraft UK
39 Walnut Tree Lane
Sudbury
Suffolk CO10 6BF

WOOD-TURNING LATHE
Record Power
Parkway Works
Sheffield S9 3BL

MECHANICAL PARTS, PULLEYS, AXLES AND WHEELS
Meccano
Atlascraft
Ludlow Hill Road
West Bridgford
Nottingham NG2 6HD

Also available from most hobby shops.

INDEX

ACKNOWLEDGEMENTS

My three children, Polly, William and James, have been the inspiration and the justification for most of the toys in this book. Their excitement and pleasure have been the best reason for making these toys. So I must thank them for that excitement, and for lending me their presents to use in the book.

Thank you, too, to Duncan Peters, for letting me use his speedy green racer, and to Cliff Richards. Cliff worked diligently with me on the aeroplane, and it is his design.

I would like to express my gratitude to Rachel Smyth for designing the book and Ray Barnett for the art direction,

Richard Dawes for editing it and Theo Bergström for taking the photographs.

I am also grateful to Polly Buchanan and Alyx Chalk, who both helped in painting the toys, and to Polly Powell and Barbara Dixon for their enthusiasm.

My thanks to Elizabeth, always my best partner.